101 Ways to Prepare Curries

By
Aroona Reejhsinghani

PUSTAK MAHAL®
Delhi•Mumbai•Bangalore•Patna•Hyderabad

 *Publishers*
Pustak Mahal, Delhi-110006

Sales Centres
- 6686, Khari Baoli, Delhi-110006, *Ph:* 23944314, 23911979
- 10-B, Netaji Subhash Marg, Daryaganj, New Delhi-110002
  Ph: 23268292, 23268293, 23279900 • *Fax:* 011-23280567
  E-mail: rapidexdelhi@indiatimes.com

Administrative Office
J-3/16 (Opp. Happy School), Daryaganj, New Delhi-110002
Ph: 23276539, 23272783, 23272784 • *Fax:* 011-23260518
E-mail: info@pustakmahal.com • *Website:* www.pustakmahal.com

Branch Offices
BANGALORE: 22/2, Mission Road (Shama Rao's Compound),
          Bangalore-560027, *Ph:* 22234025 • *Fax:* 080-22240209
          E-mail: pmblr@sancharnet.in • pustak@sancharnet.in

MUMBAI: 23-25, Zaoba Wadi (Opp. VIP Showroom),
          Thakurdwar, Mumbai-400002
          Ph: 22010941 • *Fax:* 022-22053387
          E-mail: rapidex@bom5.vsnl.net.in

PATNA: Khemka House, 1st Floor (Opp. Women's Hospital),
          Ashok Rajpath, Patna-800004
          Ph: 3094193 • *Telefax:* 0612-2302719
          E-mail: rapidexptn@rediffmail.com

HYDERABAD: 5-1-707/1, Brij Bhawan, Bank Street, Koti,
          Hyderabad-500095, *Telefax:* 040-24737290
          E-mail: pustakmahalhyd@yahoo.co.in

© Pustak Mahal, 6686, Khari Baoli, Delhi-110006

I.S.B.N. 81-223-0018-9

Edition : 2005

Printed at : Hi-Zeal Graphics, Delhi.

CONTENTS

4

5

INTRODUCTION

India is famous for its curries. In fact, it is the home of an endless variety of curries, each better than the other. Indians relish hundreds of curries made with vegetables, meat, fish, prawn and eggs. Every State in India has its own special way of preparing curries, therefore, each curry has a unique flavour. For example, in Southern India, curries are made with coconut, as their base. And in Kerala where coconut grows in abundance, coconut oil is also used for cooking. Bengal specializes in fish curries prepared in mustard oil. In Punjab, which is greatly influenced by Mughal cuisine, one comes across many exotic curries prepared with onion and tomatoes as a base. In Punjabi curries, coconut is rarely used. Curries are always served with plain fluffy boiled rice and papads which are either fried or roasted.

In India, majority of the people are vegetarian, hence there is a greater variety of delicious vegetarian curries prepared with dals and a variety of vegetables, curds and buttermilk. But this does not mean that there is very little to choose in case of non-vegetarian curries. Indian meat curries, in fact, take many forms. Like kofta curries, ground meat is shaped into balls and cooked in a deliciously rich sauce or curry. Then, there are korma curries — spicy and delicious, keema curries — which is ground meat cooked with peas and decorated with hard-boiled eggs.

In this book, I have chosen for you a wide variety of flavours — some simple, some exotic, some extraordinarily delicious. This book contains recipes for some special curries made and enjoyed in every part of India. The aim is to make people relish curries of a particular region even if they don't belong to that region. Even the foreigners can try these recipes to relish a unique taste. Here for you is a distinctive selection of curries which are as distinctive as different wines in different bottles.

Aroona Reejhsinghani
502 B, Lila Apts.
opp. Gul Mohar Gardens,
Yari Road, Versova
Bombay-61
Ph – 6360224

1

PUNJABI CURRIES

Punjabis are acclaimed as gourmets the world over. Their fondness for rich food has led to the development of an abundant variety of spicy and colourful curries. In Punjabi curries, vegetables do play an important role, therefore many of their vegetarian curries are quite unique. Some curries are particular to Punjab, like pakoda curry which is prepared by cooking round fluffy balls of gramflour in a rich yellow curd curry. Non-vegetarian Punjabi curries mostly comprising fish, chicken and mutton have distinct Mughlai influence on them in appearance and taste. They will satisfy any gourmet.

VEGETARIAN CURRIES

BESAN KOFTA CURRY

Ingredients (Serves 4)

- 1 large onion
- 4 flakes of garlic
- 2 big tomatoes, pureed
- 1 tsp. garam masala
- 1/4 tsp. turmeric powder
- 1 tblsp. dhania-jeera powder
- Salt and chilli powder to taste

For Koftas

- 250 grams besan or gram flour
- 1/2 tsp. cumin seeds
- $1\frac{1}{2}$ tblsps. melted ghee
- 1 tsp. crushed pomegranate seeds
- 100 grams grated onions
- Alubhukharas or dry plums, seeded

Preparation

Mix together all the kofta ingredients except plums, without adding water. Turn the ingredients paste into balls around the whole plums. Deep fry the balls to a golden colour. Grind onion and garlic to a paste. Heat 2 tbslps. ghee and fry the ground paste to a golden colour. Add to the paste all the spices and tomatoes and cook till the ghee separates. Then add 2 cups of water, bring slowly to a boil and keep boiling gently for 5 minutes. Then add koftas and boil for 5 more minutes. Serve hot decorated with coriander leaves.

DAHI KOFTA CURRY

Ingredients (Serves 6)

- 2 large tomatoes, pureed
- 1 large onion
- 8 flakes of garlic
- 1/4 coconut
- 1 tblsp. dhania-jeera powder
- 1/4 tsp. turmeric powder
- Handful of coriander leaves
- Salt and chilli powder to taste

For Koftas

- 250 grams curd
- 50 grams gramflour or besan
- 25 grams mixed finely sliced nuts like almonds, raisins, cashewnuts, walnuts, pistachios
- 1 tsp. grated ginger
- 1/4 tsp. garam masala
- Handful of chopped coriander leaves
- Salt , lime juice and chilli powder to taste

Preparation

Grind nuts, ginger and coriander leaves to a paste. Mix with garam masala, salt and lime juice and set aside. Put curd in a clean piece of cloth and tie loosely. Hang the bag for a couple of hours to make all the liquid drip through. Mix salt, curd and gramflour, and knead to a smooth mixture. Form the mixture into small balls around the ground paste made earlier. Deep fry the balls to golden colour. Grind onions, garlic and coconut to a paste. Heat 4 tblsps. ghee and fry the paste to a golden colour. Add to the fried paste, spices and tomatoes and cook till ghee separates. Then add 2 cups of water, bring the mixture to a boil, and keep boiling for 5 minutes. Now put in koftas, reduce heat to simmering and boil for 5 more minutes. Decorate with chopped coriander leaves.

BHIEN CURRY

Ingredients (Serves 4)

- 250 grams bhien or lotus stems
- 250 grams peas, boiled
- 100 grams tomatoes, pureed
- 4 flakes of garlic, 1 large onion
- 1 tblsp. dhania-jeera powder
- 4 green slit chillies
- Handful of coriander leaves
- A few curry leaves
- 1/4 tsp turmeric powder
- 1/4 tsp. garam masala
- Salt and chilli powder to taste

Preparation

Clean, wash, slice and boil bhien. Grind onion and garlic to a paste. Heat 3 tblsps. ghee and fry the paste to a golden colour. Add tomatoes, spices, curry leaves and chillies to the fried paste and cook till the ghee separates. Then add vegetables, mix well and then pour in the coconut milk. Simmer over a gentle fire till the curry turns a little thick. Decorate with chopped coriander leaves.

BHIEN KOFTA CURRY

Ingredients (Serves 5)

For Koftas

- 250 grams bhien, cleaned, sliced and boiled
- 1 small onion minced
- Handful of coriander leaves
- 2 green chillies, minced
- 3 tblsps. gramflour or besan
- A few mint leaves
- 1/2 tsp. ground cumin seeds
- Salt and chilli powder to taste

For Curry

- 2 big onions
- 8 flakes of garlic
- 4 big tomatoes
- 3 tblsps. beaten cream
- 1/4 tsp. turmeric powder
- 1 tblsp dhania-jeera powder
- Handful of coriander leaves
- Salt and chilli powder to taste

Preparation

Grind bhien to a smooth paste. Mix in all the kofta ingredients and form into small balls. Deep fry to a golden colour. Grind onion and garlic to a paste. Heat 3 tblsps. ghee and fry the paste to a golden colour. Add to the golden paste, spices and tomatoes and cook till the ghee oozes out. Then add 2 cups of water. Bring the mixture to a boil, reduce heat and put in the koftas. Boil over a slow fire for 5 minutes. Mix in cream and decorate with coriander leaves. Serve hot.

PUMPKIN KOFTA CURRY

Ingredients (Serves 6)

For Curry

- 2 cups coconut milk
- 1 cup nicely beaten curd
- 100 grams grated tomatoes
- 1 tsp. each of ginger and garlic paste
- 1 big onion, grated
- 1/2 tsp. garam masala
- 1 tblsp. dhania-jeera powder
- 1/4 tsp. turmeric powder
- Handful of coriander leaves
- Salt and chilli powder to taste

For Koftas

- 1/2 kilo peeled and grated pumpkin or doodhi
- 3 tblsps. wheat flour
- 1 small onion, minced
- 1/2 tsp. minced ginger
- 2 green chillies, minced
- Handful of sliced coriander leaves
- Salt and chilli powder to taste

Preparation

Squeeze out water from pumpkin. Mix it in all the kofta ingredients and form into balls. Deep fry the balls to a golden colour. Heat 3 tblsps. ghee and fry ginger, garlic and onions to a golden colour. Add to it tomatoes and spices and fry till the ghee oozes out. Mix in curd and coconut milk, heat gently, add koftas and simmer gently for a few minutes. Decorate with coriander leaves.

PAKODA CURRY

Ingredients (Serves 6)

For Curry

- 1/2 kilo sour curd
- 1/4 tsp. each of fenugreek, mustard and cumin seeds
- Dash of asafoetida
- 6 green slit chillies
- 1/2 tsp. turmeric powder
- A couple of curry leaves
- 1 tblsp. minced ginger
- 1 medium onion, minced
- 2 tblsps. gramflour or besan
- 1 large tomato, sliced
- Salt to taste

For Pakodas

- 100 grams gramflour or besan
- 1 tblsp crushed pomegranate seeds
- A few sliced mint leaves
- 2 green chillies minced
- 1 tsp. ginger minced
- 1 small potato, 1 small cauliflower, 1 small carrot
- 2 tblsps. boiled peas
- Salt to taste
- A pinch of soda bicarbonate

Preparation

Chop the vegetables very finely. Mix all the pakoda ingredients together along with enough water to form thick batter. Drop teaspoonfuls of batter in smoking ghee and fry to a golden colour. Heat 3 tblsp. ghee and fry mustard, fenugreek, cumin seeds and hing. Add onion, ginger, curry leaves and fry till soft. Add tomatoes, spices and salt. Fry till the ghee oozes out, then put in curd beaten with 4 cups water and mixed with gramflour. Add salt, turmeric and chillies. Bring slowly to a boil, reduce heat and simmer gently for 5 minutes Now add pakodas. Simmer till curry turns a little thick. Decorate with coriander leaves, and sprinkle garam masala on top.

ZAMIKAND KOFTA CURRY

Ingredients (Serves 5)

For Koftas

- 250 grams Zamikand or yam
- 100 grams paneer
- 2 tblsps. cornflour
- 1 tblsp. mango powder
- Handful of coriander leaves
- 2 green chillies, minced
- 1/2 tsp. grated ginger
- Salt to taste

For Curry

- 3 big tomatoes, grated
- 2 tblsps. powdered cashew nuts
- 1 onion, grated
- 1 tsp. each of grated ginger and garlic.
- Handful of chopped coriander leaves
- 2 tblsps. cream
- 1/2 tsp. garam masala
- 1/4 tsp. turmeric powder
- 1 tblsp. dhania-jeera powder
- Salt and chilli powder to taste

Preparation

Boil zamikand, mash it to a paste and mix with cornflour and salt. Mix the remaining kofta ingredients with paneer. Divide zamikand into small portions and form into koftas or balls around the paneer mixture. Deep fry the balls to a golden colour. Heat 3 tblsps. oil and fry onions, ginger and garlic till soft. Add to the fried contents tomatoes, salt, spices and cashewnuts. Keep frying till the oil comes out. Then add 2 cups water. Cook for two minutes, then mix in the cream and pour the mixture over the koftas. Sprinkle garam masala on top and decorate with coriander leaves.

Mushroom Curry

Ingredients (Serves 4)

- 250 grams mushrooms, cut into four pieces each
- 50 grams powdered cashewnuts
- 5-6 almonds, blanched and sliced
- 250 grams peas, boiled
- 2 tblsps. khoya
- 1 cup grated coconut
- 1/2 cup cream
- 1 tomato grated
- 8 flakes of garlic, 1/2 inch piece ginger
- 4 green chillies
- 4 cardamoms, 4 cloves
- 50 grams paneer, cubed
- 1/4 tsp. turmeric powder
- Handful of chopped coriander leaves
- Salt and chilli powder to taste

Preparation

Fry khoya to a brown colour. Also fry mushrooms to a golden colour. Fry paneer. Grind coconut, ginger, garlic and chillies and coriander to a paste. Heat 4 tblsps. ghee and add cardamoms and cloves, then put in the ground tomato paste and cook till the ghee comes out of the mixture. Now put in khoya, cashewnuts, spices, mushrooms and mix the contents with 2 cups water. Cook till the gravy is reduced to half. Add peas, paneer and cream, and remove from fire after a few minutes. Decorate with almonds.

BANANA KOFTA CURRY

Ingredients (Serves 4)

For Koftas

- 6 raw bananas
- 1 tsp. grated ginger
- Handful of coriander leaves, ground
- 2 green chillies, ground
- 2 tblsps. cornflour
- 100 grams khoya
- 1 tblsps each of chopped cashewnuts and raisins
- 1/4 tsp. garam masala
- Salt to taste

For Curry

- 4 cloves, 4 cardamoms, 2 bay leaves
- 100 grams onions, grated
- 1 tsp. each of ginger and garlic paste
- 3 big tomatoes, grated
- 2 tblsps. ketchup
- 1/4 cup cream
- 1 tblsp dhania-jeera powder
- 1/4 tsp. turmeric powder
- Salt and chilli powder to taste

Preparation

Boil bananas and mix them with ginger, coriander leaves, green chillies and cornflour and salt. Knead these contents to a paste. Now mix together khoya, cashewnuts, raisins and garam masala. Make banana paste into balls around khoya mixture. Deep fry the balls to a golden colour. Heat 3 tblsps. ghee and add all the spices. Add ginger, garlic and onions and fry till soft. Add tomatoes, ketchup and spices. When the oil oozes out, put in 2 cups water. Boil for 10 minutes; mix in cream and pour over the koftas. Decorate with coriander leaves.

CORN KOFTA CURRY

Ingredients (Serves 4)

For Koftas

- 4 cups grated corn
- 1 cup milk
- Handful of chopped coriander leaves
- 2 green chillies, minced
- 1/4 tsp. grated ginger
- 2 tblsps. cornflour
- 100 grams grated cheese
- Salt and pepper to taste

For Curry

- 4 cloves, 4 cardamoms, 1 bay leaf
- 1/4 coconut, grated
- 25 grams groundnuts
- 1 tblsps. til
- 4 red kashmiri chillies
- 100 grams tomatoes, grated
- Handful of coriander leaves
- 1/4 tsp. turmeric powder
- 1 tblsp. dhania-jeera powder
- Salt to taste

Preparation

Fry corn in 1 tblsp. butter. Add the remaining kofta ingredients except cornflour and cheese. When the mixture turns completely dry, add cornflour and cheese. Form the mixture into small balls or koftas and deep fry the balls to a golden colour. Roast coconut, groundnuts, chillies and til and grind to a paste. Heat 4 tblsps. ghee, add the whole spices. Then add onion, ginger and garlic and fry till soft. Add coconut paste and all the spices and tomatoes and fry. When the oil comes out, put in 2 cups water. Bring to a boil, then reduce heat and cook for 5 minutes. Now pour the mixture over the koftas and decorate with coriander leaves.

CAULIFLOWER KOFTA CURRY

Ingredients (Serves 5)

For Koftas

- 1/2 kilo cauliflower, grated
- 4 tblsps. gramflour
- 1/2 tsp. cumin seeds,
  1/2 tsp. grated ginger
- Handful of chopped coriander leaves
- 2 green chillies, minced
- Salt to taste

For Curry

- 250 grams grated tomatoes
- 250 grams green peas, boiled
- 1/2 tsp. cumin seeds
- 1 tsp. ginger strips
- 1 tblsp dhania-jeera powder
- 4 green chillies, slit
- 4 tblsps. cream
- 1/4 tsp. turmeric powder
- Salt and chilli powder to taste

Preparation

Mix all the kofta ingredients together. Form into small balls and deep fry the balls to a golden colour. Heat 4 tblsps. ghee, add cumin seeds, when they stop popping, add tomatoes, ginger, spices, salt and chillies. Cook the contents till the oil comes out. Now put in peas and 2 cups water. Boil for 10 minutes. Mix in cream and pour the mixture over the koftas. Decorate with coriander leaves.

NON-VEGETARIAN CURRIES

FISH CURRY

Ingredients (Serves 4)

- 500 grams any white flesh fish like pomfret
- 250 grams tomatoes, pureed
- 1 medium onion, grated
- 6 flakes of garlic, grated
- 4 red and 4 green chillies
- 1 tsp. each of cumin and coriander seeds
- 1 tsp. garam masala
- 1/2 tsp. turmeric powder
- Salt to taste

Preparation

Clean the fish, cut it into slices and fry to a golden colour. Grind together chillies, cumin and coriander seeds, onion and garlic to make paste. Heat 2 tblsps. ghee and fry the ground paste; when it starts changing colour, add tomatoes, remaining spices and salt. Cook till the ghee oozes out, add fish and 2 cups of water. Cook the contents over a slow fire till the gravy becomes a little thick. Remove from fire and sprinkle on top garam masala and coriander leaves.

FISH KOFTA CURRY

Ingredients (Serves 5)

For Koftas

- 500 grams any white flesh fish boiled and flaked
- 1 onion, grated
- 1 tsp. each of grated ginger and garlic
- 3 slices of bread, soaked in water and squeezed dry
- Handful of coriander leaves
- 4 green chillies, minced
- 1 tsp. dhania-jeera power
- 1/2 tsp. garam masala
- Salt and chilli powder to taste

For Curry

- 100 grams onions, grated
- 1 tsp. each of ginger and garlic paste
- 250 grams pureed tomatoes
- 1/2 cup curd
- Handful of chopped coriander leaves
- 1/4 tsp. turmeric powder
- 1 tsp. dhania-jeera powder
- 1 tsp. garam masala
- Salt and chilli powder to taste

Preparation

Mix together all the kofta ingredients and form into round balls. Deep fry to a golden colour. Heat four tblsps. ghee and fry the paste to a golden colour. Add tomatoes and curd, spices and salt. When the ghee oozes out, add 2 cups of water. Bring the contents to a boil then reduce heat, add koftas and cook for 5 minutes. Decorate with coriander leaves and garam masala.

2

CURRIES OF UTTAR PRADESH

Among the Indian states, Uttar Pradesh has the highest population. Hindus and Muslims form two main communities of this state. Both these communities have influenced each other's food preparations and habits. The Muslim influence is quite marked on the non-vegetarian curries, which are generally prepared from mutton and chicken. But whether the curries are non-vegetarian or vegetarian, they are absolutely delicious. And, if eaten once cannot be easily forgotten.

VEGETARIAN CURRIES

DAHIWALI CURRY

Ingredients (Serves 6)

For Besan Wadies

- 250 grams besan or gramflour
- 50 grams ghee
- 100 grams curd
- 1 tblsp. poppy seeds
- 1/2 tblsp. crushed pomegranate seeds
- 1 tsp. grated ginger
- 2 green chillies, minced
- Handful of coriander leaves
- Salt and chilli powder to taste

For Curry

- 2 big cups curd beaten with 1 cup water
- 1/2 tsp. cumin seeds
- 1/4 tsp. turmeric powder
- Handful of coriander leaves
- 4 green chillies., slit
- 1 tblsp. dhania-jeera powder
- 1 inch piece ginger cut into strips
- Salt to taste

Preparation

Mix all the wadi ingredients together and form a dough. Roll out the dough into a 1/8th of an inch thick sheet. Cut the sheet into diamond shapes and deep fry to a golden colour. Heat 2 tblsps. oil and add cumin seeds and ginger. When the seeds stop tossing, add the wadies, chillies and all the spices. Mix well and then pour in the curd. Simmer for 10 minutes, sprinkle garam masala and coriander leaves on top. Serve hot.

MANGO CURRY

You can prepare this curry either from fresh mango juice or raw mango juice depending upon your choice.

Ingredients (Serves 8)

- 1 kilo mango juice of either raw or ripe mangoes
- 250 grams besan or gramflour
- 1 tsp. cumin seeds, 1/2 tsp. grated ginger
- A big pinch of asafoetida
- 1/2 tsp. black salt
- Handful of chopped coriander leaves
- 1 tblsp. dhania-jeera powder
- 1/2 tsp. shahjeera, or black jeera
- A pinch of soda bicarbonate
- Salt and chilli powder to taste
- 2 broken red chillies

Preparation

Mix besan with shahjeera, soda, black salt, ginger along with enough juice to form a thick batter. Heat enough ghee for deep frying to smoking. Lower the heat and drop the besan with the help of a teaspoon into the ghee. Deep fry the pakodas to a golden colour. Heat 2 tblsps. ghee and add asafoetida, cumin seeds and red chillies; when the seeds stop tossing, add pakodas and spices, pour in the mango juice. Cook for 5 minutes. Sprinkle on top, garam masala and coriander leaves.

BESAN KI CURRY

Ingredients (Serves 6)

For Wadies

- 250 grams besan
- 50 grams curd
- 50 grams ghee
- 1/2 tsp. crushed pomegranate seeds
- 1 tsp. ginger paste
- Handful of coriander leaves
- 1 tblsp. minced green chillies
- Salt and chilli powder to taste
- 1/2 tsp. each of crushed peppercorns, coriander and poppy seeds

For Curry

- 12 flakes of garlic, ground to a paste
- 1/2 tsp. mustard seeds
- 1 big tomato grated
- Handful of coriander leaves
- 1 tblsp. dhania-jeera powder
- 1/4 tsp. turmeric powder
- Salt and chilli powder to taste

Preparation

Mix all the wadi ingredients together. Add enough water to form a stiff dough. Roll the dough into long rolls. Boil the rolls in water for half an hour. Remove rolls from water and cut into round pieces. Heat 2 tblsps. ghee and add mustard seeds; When the seeds stop popping, add garlic, fry lightly and then add tomatoes, all the spices and salt. When the ghee oozes out, add wadies, mix well, add water in which the wadies were boiled. Cook till it becomes a little thick. Decorate with coriander leaves.

Karela Curry

Ingredients (Serves 5)

- 250 grams karela or bittergourds, peeled and sliced
- 100 grams tomatoes, grated
- 3 tblsps. besan or gramflour
- 1/2 tsp. cumin seeds
- 4 green chillies, slit
- Handful of coriander leaves
- 1 tblsp dhania-jeera powder
- 1 tsp. ginger strips
- 1/4 tsp. turmeric powder
- A big pinch of asafoetida
- Salt and chilli powder to taste

Preparation

Apply salt on karelas and set aside for a few hours. Then wash salted karelas in 3-4 changes of water. Deep fry karelas to a golden colour. Dissolve besan in 1 glass water. Heat 2 tblsps. oil and add asafoetida, ginger and cumin seeds. When the seeds stop tossing, add tomatoes and chillies, all the spices and salt. Cook till the oil comes out. Then add vegetables and besan. Cook till the curry becomes a little thick. Decorate with coriander leaves.

POTATO KOFTA CURRY

Ingredients (Serves 5)

For Koftas

- 250 grams potatoes, boiled, peeled and mashed
- 2 tblsps. cornflour
- For filling: 125 grams coarsely chopped boiled peas, 1 tblsp each of sliced cashewnuts and raisins
- 1/4 tsp. grated ginger
- 1/4 tsp. garam masala
- 2 green chillies, minced
- 2 tblsps. grated coconut
- Handful of finely sliced coriander leaves
- Salt to taste

For Curry

- 100 grams onions, grated
- 1/2 tsp. each grated ginger and garlic
- Handful of sliced coriander leaves
- 1/4 tsp. turmeric powder
- 1 tblsp dhania-jeera powder
- 1/2 tsp. each of cumin seeds and garam masala
- 2 tblsps. powder cashewnuts
- 2 tblsps. cream
- Salt and chilli powder to taste
- Decorate either with seedless grapes, ripe mango pieces or pineapple pieces

Preparation

Mix potatoes with cornflour and salt. Mix all the filling ingredients together. Form potato mixture into balls around the filling ingredients. Deep fry the balls to a golden colour. Now heat 3 tblsps. ghee and fry cumin seeds, then add ginger, garlic and onions and fry till the contents become soft. Then add tomatoes, spices, salt and cashewnuts. Cook till they become thick. Pour in 2 cups of water, boil for 5 minutes, mix in the cream and pour the curry over the koftas. Decorate with fruits of your choice.

Non-vegetarian Curries

Shahi Kheema Kofta Curry

Ingredients (Serves 4)

For Koftas

- 250 grams minced mutton or kheema
- 1/2 tsp. each of ginger and garlic paste
- 1/2 tsp. garam masala
- Handful of coriander leaves
- 1 egg, 2 green chillies, minced
- Salt and chilli powder to taste

For Curry

- 100 grams onions, grated
- 1 tsp. each of grated ginger and garlic
- 2 large tomatoes, grated
- 1 cup curd
- 1 tsp. garam masala
- 1 tblsp. dhania-jeera powder
- 1/4 tsp. turmeric powder
- 4 cloves, 4 cardamoms, 2 bay leaves
- 1-inch piece cinnamon stick
- Salt and chilli powder to taste

Preparation

Mix all the kofta ingredients together. Form the mixture into small balls and deep fry them to a golden colour. Heat 3 tblsps. ghee, add to it whole spices, then ginger, garlic and onions. Fry till the whole thing becomes soft. Add tomatoes, curd and spices. When the oil comes out, put in koftas, pour in 2 cups water and then cook over a slow fire for 5 minutes. Decorate with coriander leaves and sprinkle garam masala on top.

NAWABI KABAB CURRY

Ingredients (Serves 4)

For Kababs

- 250 grams minced mutton or kheema
- 100 grams chana dal
- 1 onion, 1/2 tsp. ginger and garlic paste
- Handful of coriander leaves
- 2 green chillies, minced
- 2 small eggs
- 1 tsp. garam masala
- Salt and chilli powder to taste

For Curry

- 100 grams grated onions
- 1 tsp. grated ginger and garlic
- 250 grams grated tomatoes
- 1/2 tsp. cumin seeds
- 4 cloves, 4 cardamoms, 1 small piece cinnamon stick
- 1 tsp. garam masala
- 1 tblsp dhania-jeera powder
- Handful of coriander leaves
- Salt and chilli powder to taste

For Filling

- 1 cup curd, 2 tblsps. minced chillies
- 2 tblsps. minced onion, 1 tsp. minced ginger
- 2 tblsps. minced coriander leaves

Preparation

Boil together all the kofta ingredients except eggs in salted water till tender and completely dry. Grind to a paste and mix in the eggs. Hang curd to remove all water. Beat the curd and mix it with rest of the filling ingredients. Form mutton mixture into balls around the filling. Deep fry the balls to a golden colour. Heat 4 tblsps. ghee and add in it all the spices. Also add ginger, garlic and onions and fry till the contents turn golden. Add tomatoes, spices and salt. When the mixture turns thick, pour in 2 cups of water. Boil for 10 minutes, pour it over the koftas, and sprinkle garam masala and coriander leaves on top. Serve hot.

MIRCHIWALE GHOSHT KI CURRY

Ingredients (Serves 5)

- 500 grams mutton, cut into serving portions
- 150 grams onions, grated
- 2 cups sour curd
- 1 tblsp. each of ginger and garlic paste
- 1 tblsp. dhania-jeera powder
- 1 tsp. garam masala
- 100 grams thick green chillies
- 1 tblsp each of mustard, cumin seeds and kalonji
- 1 tblsp each of black or shahjeera
- 1/4 tsp. fenugreek seeds
- Juice of lime
- Salt and chilli powder to taste

Preparation

Grind together all the whole spices. Mix them with lime juice, salt and chilli powder. Make a slit in each chilli halfway through and fill the chillies with the mixture. Fry to a light golden colour. Mix together the remaining ingredients along with 100 grams ghee. Cook the mixture over a slow fire till the mutton is done and dry. When the ghee comes on top, add 2 cups water and put in the chillies. Cook for another 5-7 minutes. Serve hot.

KHEEMA MUTTON CURRY

Ingredients (Serves 5)

- 500 grams minced mutton kheema
- 250 grams grated onions
- 250 grams green peas
- 1 tsp. each of ginger and garlic paste
- 1 tblsp. dhania-jeera powder
- 100 grams tomatoes, grated
- 150 grams beaten curd
- A few mint leaves
- 4 hard boiled eggs, shelled and halved
- 1 tblsp. garam masala, 1/4 tsp. turmeric powder
- 1 large handful chopped coriander leaves
- Salt and chilli powder to taste

Preparation

Heat 100 grams ghee and fry onion, ginger and garlic till soft. Add kheema and fry till dry and crumbly. Then add spices, salt, curd and tomatoes. Cook the mixture till it turns dry. Add peas and cover with hot water. When the kheema is cooked, remove from fire. Sprinkle on top coriander leaves, garam masala and decorate with sliced eggs.

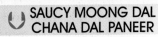

**MATAR PANEER
SHAHI KOFTA CURRY**

**SAUCY MOONG DAL
CHANA DAL PANEER**

KALEJI MASALA MUTTON KORMA

BANANA FISH CURRY VEG. MANCHURIAN

3
MAHARASHTRIAN CURRIES

Marathis are simple, hard-working and unassuming. Therefore their eating habits are also simple. Every morning one finds the lady of the house busy grinding coconut and other spices on the grinding stone. Although it is a laborious task, Marathi women do not mind it because without the addition of coconut and hot and spicy condiments no Marathi curry is said to be complete. Marathis are very fond of fish and shellfish, therefore prawn and fish curry take a place of pride on their menu. Pomfret and bangda are the most popular fishes of Maharashtra. Maharashtrians are so obsessed with fish that they buy fish and dry it in the sun in summer so that they can have fish curry in the monsoons and also when heavy rains prevent the fishermen from bringing in the fresh catch.

NON-VEGETARIAN CURRIES
SPICY POMFRET CURRY

Ingredients (Serves 4)

- 1 pomfret, cleaned and cut into slices
- 1/4 coconut
- 4 green chillies
- 1-inch piece of ginger
- 4 flakes of garlic
- 1/2 small bunch of coriander leaves
- 1/2 tsp. turmeric powder
- 1 small ball of tamarind
- 1/2 tblsp. ground cumin seeds
- 1/2 tblsp. ground coriander seeds
- Salt and chilli powder to taste

Preparation

Soak tamarind in $1\frac{1}{2}$ cup hot water for 5 minutes then squeeze out the juice, grind the remaining ingredients to a paste and apply paste on the fish. Heat 3 tblsps. oil and fry the fish nicely then pour in the tamarind water and cook till the gravy is a little thick.

FISH AND POTATO CURRY

Ingredients (Serves 5)

- 1 medium pomfret, cleaned and sliced
- 2 medium potatoes, peeled and diced into cubes
- 1 big onion, minced
- 1/4 tsp. turmeric powder
- 1 tblsp. dhania-jeera powder
- 1/4 coconut
- 2 big tomatoes, pureed
- 4 green chillies, slit
- A few curry leaves
- 2 tblsps. tamarind water
- Salt and chilli powder to taste

Preparation

Grind coconut to a paste. Heat 3 tblsps. oil and fry the onions till they become soft. Add tomatoes, coconut, spices and chillies. When the tomatoes turn soft, add potatoes, pour in two cups of water and cook till the potatoes are half done. Lightly fry the fish and add to the curry. Add curry leaves and tamarind. Cook till the potatoes and fish are done. Decorate with coriander leaves.

BANGDA CURRY

Ingredients (Serves 6)

- 1 dozen bangda fish
- 1/4 coconut
- 6 green chillies
- 8 flakes of garlic
- 1 lime-sized ball of tamarind
- 4 flakes of garlic, sliced finely
- Handful of coriander leaves
- 1/4 tsp. turmeric powder
- 1 tblsp. dhania-jeera powder
- Salt and chilli powder to taste

Preparation

Cut the fishes after cleaning them into small pieces. Apply on the cut pieces salt, chilli, and turmeric powder. Soak tamarind in two cups of water for 5 minutes and then squeeze out the juice. Grind coconut, chillies and whole flakes of garlic to a paste. Heat 4 tblsps. oil and fry the sliced garlic to a red colour. Add to it fish and fry a little, then add ground paste and spices, mix well. Now pour in the tamarind water. Cook till done. Serve decorated with chopped coriander leaves.

PRAWN CURRY

Ingredients (Serves 4)

- 500 grams prawns, cleaned and deveined
- 1/2 tsp. turmeric powder
- 1/2 coconut
- 1 tsp. coriander seeds
- 6 red chillies
- 1 small onion
- 1/2 cup tamarind water
- Handful of coriander leaves
- 2 medium onions minced
- 1 tsp. ground cumin seeds
- Salt and chilli powder to taste

Preparation

Apply salt and turmeric on prawns and set aside for half an hour. Grind coconut, small onion, coriander and cumin seeds and chillies to a paste. Heat 4 tblsps. oil and fry onions till soft. Add prawns and fry till they turn dry. Pour in 1 cup water with tamarind and cook till the prawns are almost done, then put in the ground paste and cook till prawns are done. Serve decorated with coriander leaves.

Prawns and Vegetable Curry

Ingredients (Serves 8)

- 500 grams prawns, shelled and deveined
- 2 medium onions, minced
- 2 medium potatoes, peeled and cubed
- 250 grams peas, shelled
- 1 small brinjal, diced
- 1 drumstick, scraped and cut into 1-inch pieces
- 2 medium tomatoes, blanched and sliced
- 8 cocums
- 4 green chillies
- 1 small bunch of coriander leaves
- 1/4 coconut
- 1 tblsp. each of grated garlic and ginger
- 1 tsp. each of garam masala and turmeric powder
- 2 tblsp. dhania-jeera powder
- Salt and chilli powder to taste

Preparation

Grind chillies, coriander leaves, coconut, garlic and ginger to a paste. Apply salt and turmeric on prawns and set aside for half an hour. Clean and wash the cocums. Heat 5 tblsps. oil and fry the onions till soft. Add prawns and fry till dry. Then mix in the vegetables, ground coconut paste, salt and spices. When the vegetables are almost done, put in tomatoes and cocums. When the vegetables are cooked, remove from fire and decorate with coriander leaves.

PRAWN AND PUMPKIN CURRY

Ingredients (Serves 8)

- 500 grams prawns, shelled and deveined
- 500 grams red or white pumpkin, diced
- 6 red chillies
- 1 tsp. fenugreek seeds
- 1 tblsp coriander seeds
- 1 medium onion
- 1 small onion, finely sliced
- A few curry leaves
- 6 flakes of garlic
- 1/2 tsp. turmeric powder
- 1 tsp. cumin seeds
- 1/2 coconut
- 1 lime-sized ball of tamarind
- Salt to taste

Preparation

Fry all the spices, coconut, whole onion and garlic to a red colour and grind to a paste. Cover tamarind with 1 cup hot water for 5 minutes and then squeeze out the juice. Heat 4 tblsps. oil and fry prawns till dry. Put in the pumpkin and 2 cups water and salt and cook till the prawns are almost done. Put in the tamarind and coconut paste and continue cooking till the prawns are done. Remove from fire. Heat 1 tblsp. oil and fry curry leaves and sliced onion nicely and pour it over the curry.

MUTTON CURRY

Ingredients (Serves 4)

- 500 grams mutton, cut into serving portions
- 3 medium onions, grated
- 1 tblsp. each of ground ginger and garlic
- 6 red chillies
- 1 tblsp. peppercorns

- 1/2 tsp. turmeric powder
- 1/2 dry coconut
- 1 large onion
- 1-inch piece cinnamon stick
- 1 tblsp. poppy seeds
- 4 cardamoms, 4 cloves
- Salt and chilli powder to taste

Preparation

Grind chillies, mix them with ginger, salt and turmeric powder and apply the mixture on the mutton. Set it aside for 1 hour. Roast coconut and 1 big onion on fire till red and grind to a paste along with poppy seeds and whole spices. Heat 5 tblsps. ghee and fry onions till brown, add mutton and fry to a golden colour. Mix in the coconut paste and cover with hot water. Cook till the mutton is tender. Decorate with coriander leaves.

CHICKEN AND PEAS CURRY

Ingredients (Serves 6)

- 1 medium chicken, disjointed
- 250 grams peas
- 125 grams onions, finely sliced
- 8 flake garlic
- A 2-inch piece of ginger
- 8 green chillies
- 1 tsp. garam masala

- 1 tblsp dhania-jeera powder
- 1/8 tsp. each of grated nutmeg and mace
- Handful of coriander leaves
- 1/2 tsp. turmeric powder
- 250 grams beaten curd
- 3 cups thin and 1 cup thick coconut milk
- 25 grams cashewnuts
- Salt and chilli powder to taste

Preparation

Grind ginger, garlic and chillies to a paste. Mix the paste into curd along with all the spices, salt and chicken and set aside for 1 hour. Heat 6 tblsps. oil and fry onions to a red colour. Then add chicken and fry it to a red colour. Add cashewnuts and pour in thin coconut milk. Cook over a slow fire till the chicken turns almost tender. Add peas and thick milk. Simmer over a slow fire till the chicken turns soft. Decorate with coriander leaves.

4

GUJARATI CURRIES

Since a large number of Gujaratis are vegetarian, it is not surprising to find that they prepare some of the most delicious vegetarian curries. Among the most popular Gujarati curries are sweet and sour curry and buttermilk curry. Gujaratis have endless ways of preparing curries, each different and tantalizing.

Vegetarian Curries

Lady's Finger Curry

Ingredients (Serves 4)

- 250 grams lady's fingers (bhendi), slit lengthwise, but not halved
- 1 glass buttermilk
- 2 tblsps. gramflour or besan
- 1/2 tsp. turmeric powder
- 1/2 tblsp. grated ginger
- 4 green chillies
- 1 small bunch of coriander leaves
- 4 flakes of garlic
- 1 small onion
- 1 tblsp. dhania-jeera powder
- Salt and chilli powder to taste

Preparation

Grind ginger, chillies, coriander leaves, onion and garlic to a paste. Mix the paste with spices and salt, and stuff it into each bhendi. Dissolve gramflour in buttermilk. Heat 3 tblsps. oil and fry the vegetable nicely. Put in buttermilk, salt and turmeric powder. Cook over a slow fire till the curry turns a little thick. Serve decorated with chopped coriander.

CORN CURRY

Ingredients (Serves 5)

- 4 corn cobs, 1 glass buttermilk
- 25 grams cashewnuts
- 1/4 dry coconut
- 2 medium onions
- 1/2 tsp. each of grated ginger and garlic
- 5 green chillies
- 2 medium potatoes, boiled, peeled and cubed
- 1 small bunch of coriander leaves
- 1/2 tsp. each of turmeric powder and garam masala
- 1 tsp. dhania-jeera powder
- Salt and chilli powder to taste

Preparation

Roast the coconut and grind it to a paste along with ginger, garlic, chillies, cashewnuts, onions and coriander leaves. Deep fry the potatoes to a golden colour. Heat 3 tblsps. oil and fry the ground paste till the oil floats out. Then put in the corn, all the spices and salt. Pour in the buttermilk and cook over a slow fire till the corn is done. Then put in the potatoes. Cook for a few more minutes and serve decorated with chopped coriander leaves.

CARROT KOFTA CURRY

Ingredients (Serves 6)

For Curry

- 2 big tomatoes, grated
- 1/4 coconut
- 1 tblsp. poppy seeds
- 2 tblsps. curd
- 10 cashewnuts
- 1 tsp. each of ginger and garlic paste
- 1 small onion
- 4 green chillies
- 1 small bunch of coriander leaves
- 1/2 tsp. each of turmeric powder and garam masala
- 1 tblsp garam masala
- Salt, sugar and chilli powder to taste

For Koftas

- 500 grams grated carrots
- 2 tblsps. gramflour
- 1 small bunch of coriander leaves
- 2 green chillies, minced
- 1 tsp. grated ginger
- 1 tsp. ground cumin seeds
- Raisins
- A few sliced mint leaves
- Salt and chilli powder to taste

Preparation

Grind ginger, chillies, mint and coriander leaves coarsely. Squeeze out all the moisture from carrots. Mix all the kofta ingredients except raisins. Form the carrots into oblong-shaped balls around a raisin. Deep fry the carrots to a golden colour. To prepare curry, grind coconut, poppy seeds, ginger, garlic and onions to a paste. Heat 3 tblsps. oil and fry the paste till the oil comes out. Put in all the spices, tomatoes, sugar and curds. Cook till dry. Put in 3 cups of water, boil for 5 minutes. Pour the curry over koftas and serve decorated with coriander leaves.

BRINJAL CURRY

Ingredients (Serves 4)

- 250 grams small brinjals
- 2 tblsps. gramflour dissolved in 1 glass sour buttermilk
- 4 green chillies, slit
- 1/2 tsp. cumin seeds
- Handful of coriander leaves
- Pinch of asafoetida
- 1/2 tsp. each of turmeric powder and garam masala
- 1 tsp. dhania-jeera powder
- Salt and chilli powder to taste

Preparation

Cut the brinjals into fours halfway through. Mix all the spices with salt and stuff into the brinjals. Heat 3 tblsps. oil and add asafoetida and cumin seeds. When the seeds stop popping, put in the brinjals and fry for 5 minutes, then pour in the buttermilk. Add sugar and chillies and cook till the brinjals are done. Serve decorated with coriander leaves.

BUTTERMILK CURRY

Ingredients (Serves 5)

- 2 glasses sour buttermilk
- 2 tblsps. gramflour
- 1 tblsp. grated jaggery
- 1/2 tsp. turmeric powder
- 1 tblsp. dhania-jeera powder
- A few curry leaves
- 1/4 tsp. each of mustard, cumin and fenugreek seeds
- 1 onion, grated
- 1 tsp. each of grated ginger and garlic
- 3 green chillies, slit
- 2 red chillies, broken into bits
- Salt to taste

Preparation

Mix buttermilk with gramflour, salt and all the spices. Heat 2 tblsps. oil and add a pinch of hing, mustard, cumin and fenugreek seeds and red chillies. Fry till the mixture turns brown. Add ginger, garlic, onion and curry leaves and cook till soft. Put in buttermilk along with remaining ingredients and cook till the curry turns a little thick. Serve hot.

MUKUND CURRY

Ingredients (Serves 4)

- 1-1/2 cups wheat flour
- 250 grams peas
- 100 grams tomatoes, grated
- 1 tsp. each of grated ginger and garlic
- Pinch of baking soda
- 2 bay leaves
- 1 glass sour buttermilk
- 1 tblsp dhania-jeera powder
- 1/2 tsp. each of garam masala and turmeric powder
- Handful of coriander leaves.
- 4 green chillies, slit
- 2 medium onions
- Salt and chilli powder to taste

Preparation

Mix together flour and salt. Rub in 1 tblsp ghee, and add enough water to form a stiff dough. Wash the dough in a bowl of water till the dough turns milky white. Remove the dough from water, mix in soda and flatten the dough to a thin round cake. Steam it till it turns spongy. Cut into small pieces and fry to a golden colour. Grind ginger, garlic onions to a paste. Heat 2 tblsps. oil and fry the paste along with the bay leaves till the oil comes out. Add all the spices, salt, tomatoes and peas. When the tomatoes turn soft, add buttermilk and chillies and fried pieces. Cook over a slow fire for 5 minutes. Serve decorated with coriander leaves.

POTATO KOFTA CURRY

Ingredients (Serves 4)

For Curry

- 2 small tomatoes, grated
- 250 grams beaten curd
- 1 cup coconut milk
- 1/2 tsp. each of turmeric powder and garam masala
- 1 tblsp dhania-jeera powder
- 4 green chillies, slit
- 2 medium onions
- 1 tsp. each of ginger and garlic paste
- A pinch of asafoetida
- A few curry leaves

For Koftas

- 2 big potatoes, boiled and peeled
- 1 slice of bread, soaked in water and squeezed dry
- 2 green chillies, minced
- Handful of coriander leaves
- 1 tsp. crushed pomegranate seeds
- 1/2 tsp. turmeric powder
- 50 grams gramflour
- A pinch of baking soda
- 1 tsp. ground cumin seeds

Preparation

Mix cumin powder, turmeric powder, salt and soda into the flour. Add enough water to form a thick batter. Mix potatoes with chillies, bread, pomegranate seeds and then form the mixture into small balls. Dip the balls in batter and deep fry them to a golden colour. Beat curd with 2 cups of water. Grind ginger, garlic and onions to a paste. Heat 3 tblsp. oil and fry the paste till the oil comes out. Add tomatoes, all the spices, curd, curry leaves and chillies. When the mixture turns dry, add pakodas and then coconut milk. Simmer for 5-7 mins. Serve decorated with coriander leaves.

TOMATO CURRY

Ingredients (Serves 6)

- 500 grams tomatoes, grated
- 2 cups thin and 1 cup thick coconut milk
- A few curry and coriander leaves
- 1/2 tsp. each of turmeric powder and garam masala
- 1 tblsp. dhania-jeera powder
- 1 tsp. each of grated ginger and garlic
- 1 medium onion, grated
- 4 green chillies, slit
- A pinch of asafoetida
- 1 tblsp. gramflour
- 1/4 tsp. each of mustard and cumin seeds
- 1 tblsp. sugar
- Salt to taste

Preparation

Mix gramflour in thin coconut milk. Heat 3 tblsps. oil and add hing, cumin and mustard seeds. When the seeds stop popping, add ginger, garlic and onion. Fry till soft, then put in tomatoes, curry leaves, all the spices, salt and sugar. Cook till the oil oozes out, then pour in thin milk and chillies. When the curry turns a little thick, pour in thick coconut milk and remove the curry from fire. Decorate with coriander leaves.

SWEET AND SOUR CURRY

Ingredients (Serves 5)

- 250 grams arhar or tuvar dal
- 50 grams each of suran, red pumpkin and doodhi
- 50 grams potatoes, brinjals and one raw banana
- 4 big tomatoes, grated
- 1 tblsp. grated jaggery
- 2 tblsps. thick tamarind juice
- A few curry leaves
- 1 big onion, grated; 1 tsp. grated ginger
- Handful of chopped coriander leaves
- A pinch of asafoetida
- 1/4 tsp. each of mustard and cumin seeds
- 1 tblsp. til
- 1 tblsp. grated coconut
- 1/2 tsp. turmeric powder
- 2 red and 2 green chillies
- Salt to taste

Preparation

Wash and soak dal in water for 1 hour. Drain and boil in water to which turmeric and salt has been added. When dal becomes soft, mash it to a paste. Heat 3 tblsps. oil, add mustard, cumin seeds and asafeotida. When the seeds stop popping, add ginger, onions, chillies and curry leaves and cook till soft. Cut all the vegetables, into 1-inch pieces and set aside. Put tomatoes into the onions and cook till the mixture becomes thick, then put in the vegetables, dal, tamarind, jaggery and 1 litre water. Cook till the vegetables are done. Sprinkle on top roasted til, coconut and coriander leaves. Serve hot.

5

BENGALI CURRIES

Love for music and good food is in the blood of every Bengali. A true Bengali will eat fish at least once every day. They are very fond of freshwater fish specially Rohu, Hilsa and Beckti. The Bengali preparation of fish is both creative and subversive. They pour in ginger and coriander or steam it in mustard (that tends to turn the nose into a flame-thrower) or use mustard and green chillies, or curd it or chop it, dop it, stuff it, fillet it, burn it, churn it, beat it, treat it and eat it. But whatever they do to the fish, their curries turn out a real delight to the palate along with rice. Bengalis also serve sweetmeats of which they are very fond. Besides fish curries, they also prepare many delicious vegetable curries.

VEGETARIAN CURRIES
BANANA KOFTA CURRY

Ingredients (Serves 4)

For Koftas

- 3 raw bananas
- 1 small bunch of coriander leaves
- 1 tsp. each of cumin seeds and sugar
- 1/2 tsp. each of grated garlic and ginger
- 3 green chillies
- Juice of 1/4th lime
- 1 big onion, grated
- 3 tblsps. gramflour
- Salt to taste

For Curry

- 250 grams potatoes, peeled and diced
- 1 medium onion, grated
- 1/2 cup sour curd
- 2 bay leaves
- 1/2 tsp. each of cumin seeds and turmeric powder
- 1 tsp. garam masala
- 1 tblsp. ground cumin seeds
- 4 green chillies, slit
- 1 tsp. each of grated ginger and garlic
- Handful of coriander leaves
- Salt and chilli powder to taste

Preparation

Boil and peel the bananas. Mix all the kofta ingredients together and form the resultant mixture into small balls. Deep fry the balls to a golden colour. Heat 3 tblsps. oil and put in bay leaves and cumin seeds. When the seeds stop popping, put in onions, ginger, garlic, sugar, salt and spices. Cook the contents till oil comes out. Then put in the potatoes and chillies, mix well and add curd mixed with 1 cup water. -When the potatoes are cooked, pour the curry over koftas and decorate with coriander leaves.

CABBAGE KOFTA CURRY

Ingredients (Serves 6)

For Koftas

- 1 medium head cabbage
- 1 onion, 1 tsp. grated ginger
- 2 tblsps. cornflour
- 2 green chillies, minced
- Handful of coriander leaves
- 1 small tomato, minced
- Salt to taste

For Curry

- 125 grams potatoes, peeled and cubed
- 1 cup sour curd mixed with 1 cup water
- 1 tblsp. dhania-jeera powder
- 1 tsp. garam masala, 1/2 tsp. sugar
- 1 tblsp. pure ghee
- 1/2 tsp. turmeric powder
- Salt and chilli powder to taste

Preparation

Mix together all the kofta ingredients and form the mixture into egg-shaped kofta. Deep fry the koftas to a golden brown colour. Heat 3 tblsps. oil and put in potatoes and spices. Fry the mixture to a golden colour, then put in salt, sugar and curd, and cook till the potatoes are done. Pour the curry over the koftas. Sprinkle garam masala on top. Heat ghee and pour on top before serving.

JACKFRUIT KOFTA CURRY

Ingredients (Serves 6)

For Koftas

- 500 grams raw jackfruit
- 1 big onion, grated
- 4 tblsps. gramflour
- 1 tblsp. each of coriander and mango powder
- 1 tsp. garam masala
- Salt and chilli powder to taste

For Curry

- 100 gram tomatoes, grated
- 1 cup sour curd
- 2 big onions, grated
- 1/2 tsp. turmeric powder
- 1 tsp. each of ground cumin seeds, garam masala and sugar
- 1 tblsp. coriander powder
- A few sprigs of coriander leaves
- 2 -3 bay leaves
- Salt and chilli powder to taste

Preparation

Peel and cut jackfruit into pieces and steam them till they turn soft. Then grind the steamed pieces to a paste and mix it with all the kofta ingredients. Form this mixture into small balls and deep fry them to a golden colour. Heat 3 tblsps. oil and fry bay leaves and onions to a golden colour. Then put in sugar, salt, all the spices, curd and tomatoes, and cook till the oil comes out. Now put in 2 cups of water, boil for 5 minutes, add koftas and boil for another 5 minutes. Decorate with coriander leaves.

Papaya Kofta Curry

Ingredients (Serves 8)

For Curry

- 2 medium potatoes, peeled and cubed
- 3 bay leaves
- 1 tsp. each of garam masala and sugar
- 4 red chillies
- 2 big onions
- 2 large tomatoes, grated
- 1/2 cup curd
- 1/2 tsp. cumin seeds
- 1 small piece cinnamon, 2 cardamoms, 2 cloves
- Salt to taste

For Koftas

- 1 medium raw papaya
- 1 medium green mango
- 3 tblsps. gramflour
- 3 green chillies
- 1 small bunch of coriander leaves
- 1 inch piece ginger
- A few mint leaves
- Salt to taste

Preparation

Peel and grate both mango and papaya finely and squeeze out the juice. Grind chillies, coriander, mint and ginger to a paste. Form the mixture into oblong-shaped balls and deep fry them to a golden colour. Heat 3 tblsps. oil and put in all the whole spices and onions and fry lightly. Add potatoes, fry nicely. Put in sugar, salt, tomatoes, curd with the remaining spices and cook till dry. Cover with water and cook till the potatoes are done. Pour the curry over koftas, sprinkle garam masala and coriander leaves on top. Cover and serve after 5 minutes.

Parval Dolma Curry

Ingredients (Serves 4)

- 250 grams large parvals
- 250 grams potatoes, peeled and cubed
- 2 bay leaves
- 2 medium onions, grated
- 1 tsp. each of ginger and garlic paste
- 1 tsp. each of garam masala and sugar
- 1/2 tsp. turmeric powder
- 1 tsp. coriander powder
- 1/2 cup sour curd
- Salt and chilli powder to taste

For Filling

- 250 grams small prawns, peeled and deveined
- 1 small onion, grated
- 1/2 tsp. each of ginger and garlic paste
- 1 tsp. ground cumin seeds
- 3 green chillies, minced
- Handful of chopped coriander leaves
- 1/2 tsp. turmeric powder
- Salt to taste

Preparation

Apply turmeric and salt on prawns and boil them in little water till they turn tender and dry. Grind the prawns with all the filling ingredients to a paste. Heat 2 tblsps. oil and fry the paste nicely. Now to prepare parval dolmas, make holes at both the ends of the parvals and remove the inside pith carefully so as not to break the shells. Fill the prawn mixture in parvals. Close the mouth of parval with a little paste of flour. Deep fry the parvals to a golden brown colour. Grind remaining ginger, garlic and onions to a paste put 3 cups of water in curd and beat nicely. Heat 3 tblsps. oil and add bay leaves and onion paste, spices and salt. Cook till the oil comes out. Add potatoes and fry nicely, then put in curd. When the potatoes are almost done, put in the parval dolmas. Continue cooking till the vegetables are done. Sprinkle garam masala on top and serve hot.

NON-VEGETARIAN CURRIES

HILSA CURRY

Ingredients (Serves 4)

- 500 grams Hilsa or Rohu fish
- 1 tsp. turmeric powder
- 4 red chillies
- 1-inch piece ginger
- 1 small bunch of sliced coriander leaves
- 1 tsp. shahjeera or black jeera
- 4 green chillies, sliced
- 100 grams mustard oil
- Salt to taste

Preparation

Clean and cut the fish into neat slices. Grind ginger and red chillies to a paste. Mix ginger with turmeric and salt and apply on the fish. Set aside for half an hour. Heat oil and put in shahjeera, then put in fish and fry nicely. Cover with hot water and put in the remaining ingredients. Simmer over a slow fire for 10 minutes. Serve hot.

Fish and Vegetable Curry

Ingredients (Serves 6)

- 500 grams Hilsa or Rohu fish, cleaned and sliced
- 2 medium potatoes, peeled and cubed
- 1 medium brinjal, sliced
- 100 grams parwal, peeled and sliced
- 1 tsp. cumin seeds, 2 bay leaves
- 1 tsp. turmeric powder
- 4 green chillies, minced
- A few sprigs of coriander leaves
- Salt and chilli powder to taste

Preparation

Fry fish to a golden colour. Heat 4 tblsps. oil. Add cumin seeds and bay leaves and when the seeds stop popping, add vegetables, spices and salt. Fry a little, then cover with water and cook till the vegetables are almost done. Then put in fish and chillies. Remove from fire when the vegetables are cooked. Sprinkle on top garam masala and coriander leaves.

MUSTARD FISH CURRY

Ingredients (Serves 4)

- 500 grams Hilsa or Rohu fish, cleaned and sliced
- 2 tblsps. mustard seeds
- 5 green chillies, 2 red chillies
- 1/4 tsp. turmeric powder
- 1/2 tsp. panchphoram (mixture of anise, mustard, fenugreek, cumin seeds and black jeera)

Preparation

Pound mustard and chillies to a paste. Heat 4 tblsps. oil and add red chillies and panchphoram. When the mixture turns brown, add mustard. Fry nicely. Cover with water, then add turmeric and salt, and bring the mixture to a boil. Fry the fish lightly and add to the boiling curry. Cook for 10-12 minutes or till the fish is done.

EGG AND PANEER CURRY

Ingredients (Serves 2)

- 250 grams paneer, cubed
- 4 eggs, hard-boiled
- 1 tsp. each of ginger and garlic paste
- A big pinch of sugar
- 50 grams blanched and sliced tomatoes
- 1/2 tsp. each of cumin seeds, turmeric powder and garam masala
- A few sprigs of coriander leaves
- Salt and chilli powder to taste

Preparation

Fry the eggs to a golden colour, then cut each egg into half, length-wise. Fry paneer to a golden colour. Grind onion, ginger and garlic to a paste. Heat 2 tblsps. ghee and add cumin seeds and when seeds stop popping, put in spices and onion paste. Fry till the ghee floats out. Add tomatoes, sugar and salt and continue cooking till the tomatoes turn soft. Then pour in 1-$\frac{1}{2}$ cups of water, bring the mixture to a boil and then add paneer and eggs. Boil for 5 minutes. Decorate with coriander leaves.

Egg Malai Curry

Ingredients (Serves 3)

- 6 eggs
- 3 big tomatoes, blanched and sliced
- 1 cup coconut milk
- 1 big onion, grated
- 1/2 tsp. each of ginger and garlic paste
- 1/4 tsp. sugar
- 2 medium potatoes, boiled, peeled and quartered
- 1 tsp. ground cumin seeds
- 2 bay leaves
- 1/2 tsp. each of turmeric powder and garam masala
- A few sprigs of coriander leaves
- Salt and chilli powder to taste

Preparation

Grind onion, ginger and garlic to a paste. Separate the yolks carefully from whites so as not to break them. Use the egg whites in any other preparation of your choice. Fry the potatoes to a golden colour. Also fry yolks gently on both the sides. Heat 3 tblsps. oil and add bay leaves and onion paste. When the onions turn golden, put in tomatoes, salt, sugar and all the spices. Cook tomatoes till dry, mix in potatoes and then pour in the coconut milk. Add the yolks and simmer gently for 5 minutes. Decorate with coriander leaves.

PRAWN MALAI CURRY

Ingredients (Serves 4)

- 500 grams prawns, shelled and deveined
- 2 cups coconut milk
- 50 grams beaten curd
- 100 grams small boiled potatoes, peeled and fried
- 1/2 tsp. each of turmeric powder and garam masala
- 1/2 tsp. each of ginger and garlic paste
- 2 medium onions, grated
- 1 tsp. each of sugar and ground cumin seeds
- 2 bay leaves, 3 red chillies
- A few sprigs of coriander leaves
- Salt to taste

Preparation

Fry potatoes lightly. Heat 4 tblsps. oil an dry onion paste to a golden colour. Add prawns and fry nicely. Add salt, curd, all the spices except garam masala, bay leaves and red chillies. Pour in the coconut milk and cook over a slow fire till the prawns are half done. Then put in the potatoes and sugar, and continue cooking till the prawns are done. Heat 2 tblsps. oil and toss in bay leaves and chillies. When the seeds stop popping, put into the curry. Sprinkle garam masala and coriander leaves on top. Serve hot.

6

SINDHI CURRIES

Since Sindhis lived under Muslim rule for centuries, Muslim influence on their food is predominant. It is not therefore surprising that some of their curries, specially the non-vegetarian ones, have Persian influence. But this does not mean that they do not have their own distinctive curries. Today Sindhi curry, which is made in different ways with varying ingredients, is enjoyed by people of various castes and creeds throughout India.

VEGETARIAN CURRIES

GIANTHA CURRY

Ingredients (Serves 5)

For Gianthas

- 200 grams gramflour or besan
- 1 tblsp. each of pomegranate and cumin seeds
- 4 green chillies, minced
- 1/2 tsp. ginger, minced
- 1 tblsp ghee
- Salt and chilli powder to taste

For Curry

- 1 large onion, minced
- 1/2 tsp. each of grated ginger and garlic
- 4 green chillies, minced
- 2 tblsps. mango powder
- 1 tblsp. coriander powder
- 1/2 tsp. each of turmeric powder and garam masala
- 1/2 tsp. each of cumin and mustard seeds
- A few sprigs of coriander leaves
- Salt to taste

Preparation

Mix together all the ingredients of gianthas. Add enough water to form a stiff dough. Roll the dough into a 1/4 inch thick sheet. Cut the sheet into long strips and each strip into 1-inch square pieces. Boil the gianthas in water for 20 minutes. Heat 3 tblsps. oil and fry onions, ginger, garlic and chillies till soft. Add gianthas along with the water in which they were boiled, spices and salt. Cook for a few minutes. Heat 1 tblsp. oil and fry mustard and cumin seeds. Put this oil over the curry and decorate with coriander leaves.

EGG DUMPLINGS 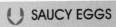 SAUCY EGGS

TORI RASBHARI 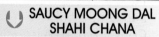 SAUCY MOONG DAL
SHAHI CHANA

GIANTHA AND SPINACH CURRY

For giantha ingredients and method of giantha preparation, refer to the recipe 'Giantha Curry'

Ingredients (Serves 4)

- 2 bunches of spinach, finely chopped
- 1 small onion, minced
- 1 tsp. each of ginger and garlic paste
- 4 green chillies, minced
- 1 tblsp. dhania-jeera powder
- 1/4 tsp. turmeric powder
- 100 grams grated tomatoes
- 6 flakes of garlic crushed
- Salt and chilli powder to taste

Preparation

Heat 3 tblsps. oil and fry onions, ginger and garlic paste and chillies till soft. Add spinach, spices, tomatoes and salt. Cook till spinach is soft. Mash the spinach mixture to a paste, add 2 cups of water and gianthas. Cook till the curry turns a little thick. Fry crushed garlic in 2 tblsps. ghee and pour the ghee over the curry.

VEGETABLE CURRY NO. 1

Ingredients (Serves 6)

- 125 grams gramflour
- 2 drumsticks, scraped and cut into big pieces
- 2 medium sized tindas, scraped and cut into quarters
- 2 medium sized potatoes, peeled and quartered
- 100 grams lady's fingers
- 50 grams each of french beans and guvar
- 1 brinjal, sliced
- 1/8 tsp. asafoetida
- 1/2 tsp. each of mustard, cumin and fenugreek seeds
- 100 grams tomatoes, grated
- 1 tsp. turmeric powder
- A few curry leaves, 1 tsp. green chilli paste
- 12-15 cocums, 1 tsp. ginger paste
- Salt to taste

Preparation

Heat 5 tblsps. oil and fry the gramflour to a golden colour. Heat 2 tblsps. oil and add asafoetida and all the seeds. When the seeds stop popping, add tomatoes, curry leaves and remaining spices. When oil oozes out, add ginger and chilli paste and all the vegetables. Fry the mixture for a few minutes. Dissolve gramflour in 1 litre water and put it in the fried mixture. Add cocums, cook till the vegetables are done and the curry is a little thick.

VEGETABLE CURRY NO. 2

Ingredients (Serves 6)

- 125 grams tuvar dal
- 3 tblsps. gramflour
- Rest of the ingredients are same as mentioned in 'Vegetable Curry No. 1"

Preparation

Boil the dal in water with salt and turmeric powder till soft. Mash the soft dal and pass it through a sieve. Dissolve gramflour in 1 litre water and pour into mashed dal. Heat 4 tblsps. ghee and add asafoetida and all the seeds. When the seeds stop popping, add tomatoes, spices and curry leaves. Let the tomatoes turn soft, then add all the vegetables and fry for a few minutes. Now put in the dal-gramflour water along with cocums. Cook till the vegetables are done and the curry turns a little thick.

NON-VEGETARIAN CURRIES

SHAHI KOFTA CURRY

Ingredients (Serves 2)

For Koftas

- 250 grams kheema or minced mutton
- 1 small onion, minced
- 3 flakes of garlic, minced
- 1/2 tsp. garam masala and cardamom seeds
- Handful of coriander leaves
- 2 green chillies, 6 mint leaves
- Salt to taste.

For Curry

- 100 grams onions, grated
- 1 tsp. grated ginger
- 4 green chillies, minced
- 100 grams tomatoes, grated
- 1 tsp. each of ground cumin seeds and garam masala
- 125 grams sour curd
- Salt and chilli powder to taste

Preparation

Grind all the kofta ingredients to a paste. Form the paste into round balls. Melt 3 tblsps. ghee in a pan, spread the koftas in it. Cover the pan, sprinkle a little cold water on the lid and cook over a slow fire till the koftas are dry. Heat 4 tblsps. ghee and fry onions, ginger and chillies till they turn soft. Then add tomatoes, all the spices, curd and salt. When the ghee oozes out, add the koftas. Pour in 2 cups of water, bring the mixture to a boil and remove it from fire. Decorate with coriander leaves.

DILPASAND KOFTA CURRY

Ingredients (Serves 2)

For Curry

- 2 medium onions, grated,
- 1 tsp. each of ginger and garlic paste
- 2 medium potatoes, boiled, peeled and quartered
- Salt and chilli powder to taste
- 1 tsp. each of coriander and cumin seeds
- 1 tsp. garam masala
- 2 red and 2 green chillies, minced
- 100 grams tomatoes, grated
- 250 grams lotus stems or bhien, cleaned, sliced and boiled

For Koftas

- 250 grams kheema
- 1 beaten egg
- Handful of coriander leaves
- 8 mint leaves
- 4 green chillies
- 1 small onion
- 1 tsp. coriander powder
- 1/2 tsp. garam masala
- 1 tsp. grated ginger
- 1 cup fine bread crumbs
- Salt and chilli powder to taste

Preparation

Boil kheema in salted water till it becomes tender and dry. Mix in kheema and rest of the kofta ingredients. Form the mixture into round balls or koftas, roll the balls in crumbs. Deep fry the balls to a golden colour. Grind onion, ginger and garlic to a paste. Heat 4 tblsps. ghee and fry the ground paste till soft. Add tomatoes, coriander leaves, chillies, all the spices and salt. Cook the mixture till the oil oozes out. Then put in 2 cups of water, potatoes and bhien. Cook for 5 minutes and pour the curry over the koftas. Sprinkle garam masala on top and serve hot.

MUTTON AND VEGETABLE CURRY

Ingredients (Serves 4)

- 500 grams mutton, cut into serving portions
- 250 grams onions, grated
- 1 tblsps. each of grated ginger and garlic
- 100 grams grated tomatoes
- 2 tblsps. coriander powder
- 1 tblsp. garam masala
- 100 grams sour curd
- 1 tsp. ground cumin seeds
- 4 green chillies, minced
- 2 medium-sized potatoes, peeled and quartered
- 250 grams lotus stems or bhien, cleaned , sliced and boiled
- 2 medium-sized tindas or white gourds, scraped and quartered
- Handful of coriander leaves
- Salt and chilli powder to taste
- 4 tblsps. brandy or whisky

Preparation

Heat 100 grams ghee and fry onions, ginger and garlic to a golden colour. Add mutton and fry to a golden colour also. Add tomatoes, spices, green chillies, curd and salt. Cook the contents till ghee comes on top, then put in all the vegetables and one glass of water and brandy. Finish cooking when both vegetables and mutton are done. Serve decorated with coriander leaves.

7

GOAN CURRIES

Goa is a tiny island lying between the Arabian Sea and the Western Ghats. Since it is skirted by the sea, it has been bestowed with abundant varieties of fish and shellfish. Goans prepare many delicious fish curries. Today throughout India, people enjoy Goan fish and prawn curries. Having lived under Portuguese rule for over 450 years, the food of Goans is a mixture of both Eastern and Western influences. Goans excel in culinary art and they make such fine chefs that most of the leading hotels in India are served by Goan chefs.

NON-VEGETARIAN CURRIES

SPICY FISH CURRY

Ingredients (Serves 4)

- 1 medium white fleshed fish, cleaned and sliced
- 1 tblsp. each of cumin seeds, coriander and poppy seeds.
- 1 tblsp. rice
- Handful of coriander leaves
- Refined flour
- 1 tblsp. grated ginger
- 12 cashewnuts, 1 tblsp. peppercorns
- 2 medium onions, finely sliced
- A big pinch of sugar
- 1/2 coconut, 6 flakes of garlic
- 4 green chillies, slit
- 4 medium tomatoes, pureed
- 1/2 tsp. turmeric powder
- Salt and chilli powder to taste

Preparation

Apply salt and turmeric powder on fish and set it aside for half an hour. Roll fish lightly in flour and fry to a golden colour. Grind coriander, cumin and poppy seeds, peppercorns, rice, coconut and cashewnuts to paste. Extract juice — this is known as thick milk. Pour 2 cups hot water over the squeezed out pulp and set it aside for 15 minutes, then squeeze the pulp dry — this is known as thin milk. Heat 3 tblsps. oil and fry onions, ginger and chillies till soft. Then put in remaining spices, tomatoes, salt and sugar. Cook till oil comes out, then put in fish and thin milk. Cook for 5 minutes, and pour in thick milk. Heat the curry to simmering and serve decorated with coriander leaves.

Pomfret Curry

Ingredients (Serves 4)

- 1 medium pomfret, cleaned and sliced
- 1/2 coconut,
- 6 red chillies, few curry leaves
- 2 tblsps. each of coriander and poppy seeds
- 1 large onion, 1 tsp. cumin seeds
- 4 green chillies, slit
- 3 cocums, 10 cashewnuts
- 6 flakes of garlic
- 1 lime-sized ball of tamarind
- Salt to taste

Preparation

Apply salt and turmeric on fish and set it aside for half an hour. Then fry the fish lightly. Roast together onion, red chillies, garlic, coconut, coriander, cumin, poppy seeds and cashewnuts along with tamarind, and grind the mixture to a paste. Heat 3 tblsps. of oil and fry the paste nicely, adding water from time to time till a nice aroma comes out of the mixture. Then pour in 3 cups of water and add cocums. Bring the mixture to a boil and put in fish and cook for 5-7 minutes. Decorate with chopped coriander leaves.

FISH AND BRINJAL CURRY

Ingredients (Serves 6)

- 1 pomfret or any other white-fleshed fish, cleaned
- 250 grams brinjals, cut into long finger-like slices
- 1 lime-sized ball of tamarind
- 1 tblsp. mustard seeds
- 1 big onion, sliced
- 1 tblsp. each of coriander and poppy seeds
- 1/2 tsp. turmeric powder, 1 tsp. cumin seeds
- 1 tblsp. each of grated ginger and garlic
- 6 red chillies
- 1 medium onion
- 1/2 coconut
- Salt to taste

Preparation

Apply salt and turmeric powder on slices of fish and set them aside for half an hour. Roast together coriander, cumin and poppy seeds, 1 medium onion, ginger, garlic, chillies and coconut. Grind this mixture to a fine paste. Fry the fish lightly in oil. Soak tamarind in one cup hot water and then squeeze out the juice. Heat 3 tblsps. oil and put in the mustard seeds, when the seeds stop popping, put in the sliced onion and fry till soft. Then put in the ground paste and fry nicely. Add brinjals, mix well, add tamarind and 3 cups of water. When the brinjals are almost done, put in the fish. Remove the curry from fire when the brinjals are done.

PORK CURRY

Ingredients (Serves 8)

- 1 kilo pork, cut into serving portions
- 5 large onions, minced
- 1/2 tsp. turmeric powder
- 2 tblsps. dhania-jeera powder
- 2-inch piece of cinnamon stick
- 8 cloves, 8 cardamoms
- 2 tblsps. peppercorns
- 1 tblsp. mustard seeds
- 10 flakes of garlic
- 2-inch piece of ginger
- 6 green chillies, slit
- 250 grams potatoes, boiled, peeled and cubed
- 1/4 cup vinegar
- Salt to taste

Preparation

Deep fry potatoes to a golden colour. Roast and grind together all spices, chillies, ginger and garlic in vinegar. Heat 6 tblsps. oil and fry the onions to a golden colour. Add pork and fry to a golden colour. Add ground paste and salt. Cover the mixture with hot water. When the pork becomes tender, mix in potatoes and remove the curry from fire. Decorate with coriander leaves.

Spicy Pork Curry

Ingredients (Serves 8)

- 1 kilo pork, cut into serving portions
- 1/4 cup vinegar
- 2 tblsps. tamarind juice
- 1 tsp. sugar
- 12 red chillies ,12 flakes of garlic
- 1 tblsp dhania-jeera powder
- 1/2 tsp. turmeric powder
- 5 big onions
- 2-inch piece of ginger
- 1 tblsp. peppercorns
- 6 green chillies, slit
- Salt to taste

Preparation

Grind 6 flakes of garlic, half the ginger, red chillies and whole spice to a paste. Heat 5 tblsps. oil and fry the onions, remaining ginger and garlic to a golden colour. Add pork, ground spices, and salt and fry the mixture nicely. Cover it with hot water and cook till the pork is done. Mix in the remaining ingredients and cook till the pork is tender. Serve hot.

CHICKEN CURRY

Ingredients (Serves 6)

- 1 medium chicken, disjointed
- 1 coconut
- 6 red chillies
- 1 tsp. each of saunf, cumin and coriander seeds
- 1/2 tsp. fenugreek seeds
- 6 flakes of garlic, 1 tblsp. peppercorns
- 2 tblsps. poppy seeds, 1/4 tsp. grated nutmeg
- 4 big onions, 2 tblsps. vinegar
- 1 small ball of tamarind
- Salt to taste

Preparation

Roast all the spices and chillies and grind them to a paste. Grate half the coconut and fry it with 2 onions and poppy seeds in oil to a golden colour and grind the mixture to a paste. Extract 2 cups thin and 1/2 cup thick milk from remaining coconut. Cover tamarind with hot water for 5 minutes, then extract its juice. Heat 2 tblsp. each of ghee and oil and fry the remaining onions to a golden colour. Add to this mixture, chicken, salt, spices and ground coconut. Mix nicely, then pour in thin milk and tamarind. Cook over a slow fire till the chicken is tender. Mix in vinegar and thick coconut milk. Decorate with coriander leaves and serve hot.

HEAD CURRY

Ingredients (Serves 4)

- 1 head of goat exclusive of brain
- 1 big onion, 1 tblsp. each of grated ginger and garlic
- 1 lime-sized ball of tamarind
- 150 grams tomatoes
- 1/2 tsp. turmeric powder
- 1 tsp. garam masala
- 6 red chillies, a few curry leaves
- 1 tblsp. dhania-jeera powder
- Salt to taste

Preparation

Clean the head inclusive of tongue, eyes, jaws and cheeks. Cut into pieces and cook adding salt. After the meat is cooked, remove skull bones. Remove skin on tongue, palate and earlobes. Cover tamarind with hot water for 15 minutes and then squeeze out its juice. Heat 4 tblsps. oil and then add the coarsely ground onions, ginger, garlic and curry leaves. Cook them till soft, then add tomatoes, all the spices and salt. When the mixture turns soft, add meat, fry nicely, then add tamarind and one cup of water. Cook for 5 minutes. Serve decorated with coriander leaves.

MUTTON CURRY

Ingredients (Serves 4)

- 500 grams mutton, cut into serving portions
- 1 coconut
- 1 tblsp. coriander seeds, 1 tsp. cumin seeds
- 10 peppercorns, 8 red chillies.
- 1 tsp. garam masala, 1/2 tsp. turmeric powder
- 1 tblsp. poppy seeds
- 1 tblsp. each of grated ginger and garlic
- 2 big onions
- Lime-sized ball of tamarind
- Salt to taste

Preparation

Grind three-fourth of the coconut and extract its thin and thick milk. Fry the remaining coconut and all the whole spices and grind them to a paste with ginger and garlic. Cover tamarind with hot water for 5 minutes and then squeeze out the juice. Heat 4 tblsp. oil and fry the onions to light golden colour. Add mutton and fry it to a red colour. Then put in ground paste and thin coconut milk and tamarind juice. Cook till the mutton is done, put in thick milk, heat and serve decorated with chopped coriander leaves.

EGG AND PEAS CURRY

Ingredients (Serves 2)

- 4 eggs
- 250 grams peas
- 5 flakes of garlic, grated
- 2 medium onions, minced
- 1 tsp. grated ginger
- 1 tsp. garam masala, 1/2 tsp. turmeric powder
- 2 medium potatoes, peeled and sliced
- 2 large tomatoes, pureed
- Handful of coriander leaves
- 4 green chillies, minced
- 3 cups thin and 1 cup thick coconut milk
- Salt and chilli powder to taste

Preparation

Heat 4 tblsps. oil and fry onions, ginger, garlic and chillies till soft. Add all the spices, salt and tomatoes and cook till oil comes out. Then add peas, potatoes and thin coconut milk. When the vegetables turn soft, pour in the thick coconut milk. Now start breaking one egg at a time into the curry after an interval of half a minute, putting each slightly away from the other. Remove the curry after boiling the eggs in it for 5 minutes. Decorate with chopped coriander leaves.

8

CURRIES OF ANDHRA PRADESH

Andhra Pradesh is the largest amongst the South Indian states. It is the largest producer of rice in India, therefore people here are very fond of rice. Andhra is also the home of chillies, both green and red varieties. Therefore, it is normal for Andhra people to use chillies liberally in their food. Besides chillies, their curries have few other spices. Hyderabad, which is Andhra Pradesh's capital, has very different cuisine. Since this city was under Muslim rule, the curries popular here have a moghlai influence. These curries are not only delicious in taste but also look nice and tempt one to have a go at them.

VEGETARIAN CURRIES

COCONUT KOFTA CURRY

Ingredients (Serves 8)

For Curry

- 500 grams tomatoes, grated
- 1 tblsp. poppy seeds
- 4 cloves, 4 cardamoms
- 1-inch piece of cinnamon
- 1/4 dry coconut
- 4 red chillies, 6 flakes of garlic
- 1-inch piece of ginger
- 1/2 tsp. turmeric powder
- 1 big onion, minced
- Handful of sliced coriander leaves
- 12 fried cashewnuts
- Salt to taste

For Koftas

- 1 big coconut
- 3 tblsps. gramflour
- 8 green chillies, minced
- 1 large bunch of coriander leaves, minced
- A big handful of mint leaves, minced
- 1 medium onion, grated
- 1/2 tblsp. each of ginger and garlic paste
- 4 ground red chillies
- 1 tsp. garam masala
- Salt to taste

Preparation

Grind the coconut coarsely and mix it and all the kofta ingredients. Form the mixture into round balls and deep fry to a golden colour. Grind all the whole spices, coconut, ginger and garlic to a paste. Heat 3 tblsps. oil and fry onions and ground paste together till the oil comes out. Add tomatoes, salt and turmeric. Cook till tomatoes turn soft, then put in 1 glass of water, bring the mixture to a boil and keep boiling for 5 minutes. Then add koftas and boil for a few more minutes. Decorate with cashewnuts and coriander leaves.

82

SWEET POTATO CURRY

Ingredients (Serves 4)

- 250 grams sweet potatoes, boiled and sliced.
- 1 medium onion, minced
- 3 green chillies, minced
- 2 big tomatoes, grated
- 1/4 tsp. turmeric powder
- 1/2 coconut, grated
- 1 tsp. cumin seeds
- 1 tblsp. coriander seeds
- 3 flakes of garlic
- A few curry leaves
- 4 red chillies
- Handful of sliced coriander leaves
- Salt to taste

Preparation

Grind coconut, red chillies, garlic, cumin and coriander seeds to a fine paste. Heat 2 tblsps. oil and fry the onions and green chillies till soft. Add tomatoes and spices and cook. When the oil comes out, add sliced sweet potatoes and ground paste. Put in 2 cups of water along with the remaining ingredients. Cook till the curry turns a little thick. Serve hot.

CHILLI CURRY

Ingredients (Serves 4)

- 24 thick and large green chillies, slit
- 1 tsp. each of ginger and garlic paste
- 2 tblsps. sesame seeds or til
- 25 raw groundnuts
- 1 tsp. cumin seeds, 1 tblsp. coriander seeds
- 1 lime-sized ball of tamarind
- 2 medium onions
- 1/4 tsp. turmeric powder
- Salt and chilli powder to taste

Preparation

Roast til, cumin and coriander seeds and powder them. Grind groundnuts coarsely. Cover tamarind with 2 cups of hot water for 5 minutes and then squeeze out pulp. Heat 2 tblsps. oil and fry onion paste to a light golden colour. Then add groundnuts and powdered spices and fry nicely. Put in the chillies and fry till they start turning brown. Pour in tamarind and cook till the gravy turns a little thick.

Cocum Kadi

Ingredients (Serves 2)

- 250 grams lady's fingers, sliced
- 12 cocums
- 3 green chillies, slit
- 1/2 coconut
- 1 medium onion, grated
- 1/2 tsp. each of ginger and garlic paste
- A few curry leaves
- Handful of coriander leaves
- 1/4 tsp. turmeric powder
- Salt and chilli powder to taste

Preparation

Fry lady's fingers to a golden colour. Extract thin and thick milk from coconut. Boil cocums and extract 1 cup juice. Heat 2 tblsps. oil and fry onion, ginger, garlic and curry leaves till soft. Add thin coconut milk, cocum juice, chillies, lady's fingers, salt and turmeric powder. Cook for 5-7 minutes. Add thick milk and coriander leaves. Serve hot.

VEGETABLE KORMA CURRY

Ingredients (Serves 4)

- 100 grams each of french beans and potatoes, sliced
- 250 grams peas
- 100 grams tomatoes, grated
- 2 cloves, 2 cardamoms, 1 small cinnamon stick
- 1/2 sp. each of ginger and garlic paste
- 1 tblsp. poppy seeds
- 2 tblsps. each of grated coconut and curd
- 1 medium onion, grated
- 4 green chillies, slit
- Handful of chopped coriander leaves
- 1/4 tsp. turmeric powder
- Salt to taste

Preparation

Grind together poppy seeds and coconut. Heat 2 tblsps. oil and add the whole spices. Then add ginger, garlic, onions and the ground paste and fry till the oil comes out. Add the remaining ingredients. When the mixture turns dry, add 2 cups of water. Cook till the vegetables are done. Decorate with coriander leaves.

MOGHLAI MALAI KOFTA CURRY

Ingredients (Serves 4)

For Koftas

- 250 grams potatoes, boiled, peeled and mashed
- 100 grams grated cheese
- 2 tblsps. cornflour, 2 tblsps. curd
- 25 grams powdered cashewnuts
- 100 grams hard slab of butter, cut into small cubes.
- Salt to taste

Fur Curry

- 100 grams onions, grated
- 1/2 tsp. each of grated ginger and garlic
- 2 large tomatoes, grated
- 1/4 tsp. turmeric powder
- 1/2 tsp. each of garam masala and dhania-jeera powder
- 50 grams cream
- 2 rings of pineapple, cubed
- A few pieces of ripe mangoes
- Salt and chilli powder to taste

Preparation

Mix together potatoes, cheese, salt and cornflour. Form the mixture into small balls around a cube of butter. Deep fry the balls to a golden colour. Heat 4 tblsps. ghee and fry onion, ginger and garlic till soft. Add curd, spices tomatoes and salt and cook till thick. Then put in 2 cups of water and cook for 5 minutes. Pour the curry over the koftas. Pour cream over top and decorate with fruits.

Non-vegetarian Curries
Murg Korma Curry

Ingredients (Serves 6)
- 1 medium chicken, disjointed
- 1/4 coconut,
- 100 grams onions, grated
- 1 cup curd
- 25 grams each of cashewnuts and charoli
- 2 tblsps. til seeds
- 1 tblsp. each of ginger and garlic paste
- 4 cloves, 4 cardamoms, 1 small cinnamon stick
- 2 bay leaves, 1/4 tsp. grated nutmeg
- 250 grams small potatoes, boiled and peeled
- 2 tblsp. lime juice
- Salt to taste

Preparation

Roast and grind together coconut, nuts and til. Mix the ground paste into the curd along with ginger, garlic and onions. Add to the mixture chicken and set aside it for 1 hour. Heat 100 grams oil and put in the whole spices. When they crackle, add the chicken along with the marinade. Cook over a slow fire till dry and the oil comes to the top. Then add the remaining spices and cover the contents with hot water. When the chicken is cooked, add lime juice and potatoes. Remove the curry from fire after a few minutes. Decorate with coriander leaves.

NIZAMI CURRY

Ingredients (Serves 4)

- 1 medium chicken, disjointed
- 250 grams onions, grated
- 2 tblsps. each of ginger and garlic paste
- 25 grams fried cashewnuts
- 25 grams blanched, sliced and fried almonds
- Handful of coriander leaves
- A few mint leaves
- 2 cups of curd
- 1 tblsp. dhania-jeera powder
- 1 tsp. garam masala
- 1/4 tsp. turmeric powder
- 4 cloves, 4 cardamoms, 1 small cinnamon stick
- Salt and chilli powder to taste

Preparation

Powder cashewnuts. Heat 100 grams ghee. Add the whole spices, when they crackle, add ginger, onions and garlic. Fry to a golden colour. Add chicken, nuts, salt and chilli powder, turmeric and dhania-jeera powder, coriander and mint and curd. Cook the mixture over a slow fire till it becomes dry and oil floats to the top. Now cover the curry with hot water and cook till the chicken is done. Sprinkle garam masala on top of curry and serve.

SHEEKH KABAB CURRY

Ingredients (Serves 4)

For Curry

- 250 grams tomatoes, grated
- 100 grams onions, grated
- 1 tsp. of ginger and garlic paste
- 1 tsp. garam masala, 1/2 tsp. cardamom powder
- 1/2 cup cream, handful of coriander leaves
- 25 grams powdered cashewnuts
- 4 cloves, 4 cardamoms, 1 small cinnamon stick
- Salt and chilli powder to taste

For Kababs

- 500 grams minced mutton or kheema
- 1/2 cup firely sliced coriander leaves
- 4 green chillies, minced
- A few sliced mint leaves
- 1 tsp. grated ginger
- 4 tblsps. oil
- 1 tsp. cardamom seeds
- 1 tsp. garam masala
- 1 medium onion, grated
- 2 tblsps. grated raw papaya with skin
- Salt and chilli powder to taste

Preparation

Mix the kabab ingredients together. Shape the mixture into long sausages or cigarette shapes on well-greased skewers. Cook the sausages over charcoal or grill until well-browned on all the sides. Remove sausages from skewers. Heat 4 tblsps. oil, add whole spices. When they crackle add onions, ginger and garlic and fry till soft. Add tomatoes, cashewnuts, salt and remaining spices. Cook till the oil separates. Then add 2 cups of water. Cook for 5 minutes and pour the curry over the kababs. Also pour cream on top and decorate with chopped coriander leaves.

9

CURRIES OF KERALA

Kerala is one of the smallest states in South India. In this state, the backwaters and canals are fringed with tall coconut palms, so the people here use fresh coconut liberally in food. A unique feature of Kerala's food is that it is the only state in India which uses coconut oil for cooking. Rice is the staple food of Keralites and it is generally served with unusually delicious curries made of jackfruit, pineapple, bananas, various vegetables and fish and seafood which are available in plenty.

VEGETARIAN CURRIES

JACKFRUIT CURRY

Ingredients (Serves 6)

- 1 medium raw jackfruit
- 1 coconut, grated
- 1 medium onion and 1 small onion, finely sliced
- 6 green chillies
- 1/4 tsp. turmeric powder
- A few curry leaves
- 1 tsp. each of cumin and mustard seeds
- Salt to taste

Preparation

Set 1/4 grated coconut aside. Extract thin and thick milk from remaining coconut. Peel the jackfruit. Grease your hands and separate the fruit. Remove seeds and cut jackfruit into pieces. Grind grated coconut, medium onion, chillies and cumin seeds to a paste. Put the jackfruit in a pan along with turmeric, salt and thin coconut milk. When the vegetable is almost done, add the ground paste and curry leaves. Continue cooking till the vegetable is done. Now mix thick coconut milk into it. Heat to simmering and remove the curry form fire. Heat 1 tblsp. of oil and put in mustard seeds, when they stop tossing, add sliced onion and fry to a light golden colour. Put fried onions in the curry and serve hot.

MANGO CURRY

Ingredients (Serves 4)

- 3 raw mangoes, peeled and sliced
- A few pods of tamarind
- 1-1/2 cups of coconut milk
- 5 red chillies
- 1/4 tsp. turmeric powder
- 1 medium onion, finely sliced
- A few curry leaves
- 1 tsp. ground cumin seeds
- Salt to taste
- Jaggery if desired

Preparation

Grind tamarind and chillies to a paste. Heat 1 tblsp. oil and fry onions till soft. Add to the fried onions, ground paste and fry nicely. Add mangoes, all the spices and salt. Pour in the coconut milk and cook till the mangoes are done. Mix in the curry, grated jaggery and curry leaves and remove it from fire.

Mixed Vegetable Curry

Ingredients (Serves 5)

- 5 cups buttermilk
- 1/2 coconut, grated
- 1 tblsp. cumin seeds
- 1-inch piece of ginger
- 4 green chillies, slit
- 4 red chillies
- 3 tblsp. gramflour or besan
- 50 grams each of potato, pumpkin, french beans
- 1 drumstick, 1 raw banana
- A few curry leaves
- 1 tsp. each of mustard seeds and urad dal
- Salt to tast

Preparation

Peel and cut all the vegetables into 1-inch pieces. Grind coconut, cumin seeds, ginger and red chillies to a paste. Blend gramflour into buttermilk. Add salt and turmeric into vegetables with very little water and cook till almost done. Then put the ground paste in the vegetables and continue cooking till the vegetables are done. Pour in buttermilk. Boil till the curry is a little thick. Heat 2 tblsps. oil and put in mustard seeds, dal and curry leaves. When the dal turns red, pour this mixture into the curry.

PINEAPPLE CURRY

Ingredients (Serves 6)

- 1 ripe pineapple
- 4 red chillies, 3 red chillies, broken
- 1/4 tsp. each of mustard and fenugreek seeds
- A few curry leaves
- 1 glass of buttermilk
- 1/2 tsp. turmeric powder
- 1/2 coconut, grated
- 1 small onion, sliced
- 1 tsp. cumin seeds
- Salt to taste

Preparation

Peel the pineapple and remove all eyes carefully. Cut into slices. Remove the inside hard portion from pineapple slices and dice into pieces. Grind coconut, cumin seeds and green chillies to a paste. Place pineapple, salt and turmeric powder in a pan with very little water. Cover the pan tightly and cook till the pineapple is almost done. Then pour in buttermilk and add the ground paste. Continue cooking till the pineapple is tender. Mix in the curry leaves and remove from fire. Heat 2 tblsps. oil and add mustard and fenugreek seeds and red chillies. When the mixture turns brown, put it into the curry.

NON-VEGETARIAN CURRIES
MUTTON KORMA CURRY

Ingredients (Serves 4)

- 500 grams mutton, cut into serving portions
- 100 grams potatoes, boiled, peeled and cut into fours
- 1/2 coconut, ground
- 1 tblsp. each of ginger and garlic paste
- 1 tblsp. green chilli paste
- 2-inch piece of cinnamon, 4 cardamoms, 4 cloves
- 1/2 cup coriander leaves, chopped
- 1/4 tsp. turmeric powder
- 100 grams curd
- Salt to taste

Preparation

Powder together the spices. Mix them into curd along with ginger, garlic and chilli paste. Apply the paste on the mutton. Heat 50 grams oil and put mutton in it. Cook over a slow fire till the mutton turns dry. Fry to a red colour. Cover the mutton with hot water, then add coriander and coconut paste, and cook till mutton is tender. Finally put in potatoes and cook for a few more minutes. Serve hot.

ALOO DUMPUKHT BRINJAL FISH CURRY
KAJU MALAI MATAR

SAAG KOFTA
SIZZLED MUTTON

RAJMAH CHICKEN CURRY
SAAG CHICKEN

COCONUT MEAT CURRY

Ingredients (Serves 4)

- 500 grams mutton, cut into serving portions
- 2 potatoes, boiled, peeled and cut into fours
- 2 medium onions, grated
- 1 tblsp. grated ginger
- 1 cup thick, 2 cups thin coconut milk
- 1/2 tsp. each of mustard and cumin seeds
- 4 cloves, 4 cardamoms
- 1 small stick of cinnamon
- 8 peppercorns, 4 green chillies, minced
- A few curry leaves
- 2 tblsps. vinegar
- Salt to taste

Preparation

Put mutton, onions, thin milk, ginger, green chillies, curry, leaves, spices, salt and vinegar in a vessel and cook till the mutton is tender. Add potatoes and thick milk and heat the mixture to simmering. Remove the curry from fire. Heat 2 tblsps. oil and fry mustard and cumin seeds. Pour the hot oil over the curry and serve hot.

CHICKEN CURRY

redients (Serves 5)

- 1 medium chicken, disjointed
- 2 large onions, grated
- 5 green chillies, minced
- 1 tblsp. grated ginger
- 1 cup thick, 2 cups thin coconut milk
- 2 tblsp. vinegar
- A few curry leaves
- 1 tblsp. coriander seeds
- 4 red chillies, 1 tblsp. peppercorns
- 1/2 tsp. each of mustard, cumin and fenugreek seeds
- 2 tsp. poppy seeds
- 1/2 tsp. turmeric powder
- 1 large onion
- 8 flakes of garlic
- 2-inch piece of cinnamon
- 3 cloves, 3 cardamoms
- 1 tsp. anise seeds
- Salt to taste

Preparation

Roast and powder together whole onion, garlic, red chillies and all the whole spices. Heat 100 grams oil and fry grated ginger, chillies and onions till soft. Add ground paste to the mixture and fry till the oil comes out. Put in chicken and cook till dry. Fry to a golden colour. Add thin coconut milk and cook till the chicken is cooked. Add thick milk, curry leaves and lime juice. Heat the curry to simmering and remove if from fire.

COCONUT FISH CURRY

Ingredients (Serves 4)

- 500 grams any white-fleshed fish, cleaned and sliced
- 2 medium onions, grated
- 1 tsp. each of ginger and garlic paste
- 4 green chillies, slit
- 1 tblsp. vinegar
- A few curry leaves
- 1/2 cup thick and 2 cups thin coconut milk
- 1/2 tsp. turmeric powder
- Salt and chilli powder to taste

Preparation

Fry the fish slices lightly. Heat 2 tblsps. oil and fry ginger, garlic and onions till soft. Add to this mixture fish and 1/2 cup of thin coconut milk, salt, vinegar and turmeric powder. Cook the contents over a slow fire till the gravy is almost dry. Pour in remaining thin coconut milk and cook till the gravy is almost thick. Finally add thick coconut milk and curry leaves. Heat to simmering and remove the curry from fire.

PRAWN AND TAMARIND CURRY

Ingredients (Serves 4)

- 500 grams prawns, cleaned, shelled and deveined
- 1 lime-sized ball of tamarind
- 1/2 coconut, 2 medium onions
- 1 tblsp. coriander seeds, 1/2 tsp. fenugreek seeds
- 8 red chillies
- A few curry leaves
- Salt to taste

Preparation

Cover tamarind with 2 cups of hot water and then squeeze out the pulp. Fry rest of the ingredients except prawns in a little oil and grind the mixture to a paste. Heat tamarind, add prawns and ground paste and cook till the prawns are done.

10

CURRIES OF TAMILNADU

Tamilnadu is populated largely with vegetarians. Therefore they prepare many delicious curries of vegetables and dals. The curries here are usually hotter than the ones prepared in the North. Generally, Tamilians use either coconut milk or coconut paste as base for their curries. Tamil curries are delightfully delicious, and with rice they make a most satisfying meal.

VEGETARIAN CURRIES

LADY'S FINGER CURRY

Ingredients (Serves 2)

- 250 grams lady's finger, sliced
- 1 big onion, grated
- 1 tsp. each of garlic and ginger paste
- 2 tblsps. grated coconut
- 4 green chillies
- Handful of coriander leaves
- 20 grams tamarind soaked in 1 cup water for 5 minutes
- 1 tblsp. dhania-jeera powder
- 1/4 tsp. turmeric powder
- 1/2 tsp. mustard seeds
- A few curry leaves
- Salt and chilli powder to taste

Preparation

Grind together onion, ginger, garlic, coconut, chillies and coriander leaves. Fry the lady's fingers to a light golden colour. Heat 2 tblsps. oil and fry the ground paste till the oil comes out. Add spices, salt and the lady's fingers. Squeeze out the tamarind water and pour into the lady's fingers along with 1/2 cup water. Cook the mixture for 5-7 minutes. Heat 1 tsp. oil and fry mustard seeds and curry leaves. Pour this oil mixture over the curry and serve hot.

BEETROOT CURRY

Ingredients (Serves 4)

- 150 grams arhar or tuvar dal
- 2 big beetroots, boiled, peeled and cubed
- 1 medium onions, grated
- 1 medium tomato, sliced
- 1 lime-sized ball of tamarind
- A few curry leaves
- 1/2 tsp. ginger and garlic paste
- 4 green chillies, slit
- 1/4 tsp. turmeric powder
- 1/2 tsp. garam masala
- Salt and chilli powder to taste

Preparation

Soak tamarind in hot water for 5 minutes, then squeeze out the tamarind water. Boil dal along with salt and turmeric powder till soft. Mash the boiled dal to a paste. Heat 2 tblsps. oil, add a pinch of asafoetida, curry leaves, ginger, garlic and onions. Fry the mixture till oil comes out. Add dal, chillies, tamarind, tomato pieces and beetroots. Cook for 10 minutes over a slow fire. Sprinkle garam masala on top.

COCONUT AND TOMATO CURRY

Ingredients (Serves 4)

- 250 grams tomatoes, grated
- 150 grams arhar or tuvar dal
- 100 grams grated coconut
- 1/2 tsp. mustard seeds
- 4 green chillies, slit
- A few curry leaves
- 1/4 tsp. turmeric powder
- 1/2 inch piece of ginger, grated
- Handful of chopped coriander leaves
- A big pinch of asafoetida
- Salt and chilli powder to taste

Preparation

Grind coconut and ginger to a paste. Boil dal in water with turmeric powder and salt till the dal becomes very soft. Mash the boiled dal to a paste. Heat 4 tblsps. oil and add mustard seeds and asafoetida. When the seeds stop tossing, add coconut paste, curry leaves. Fry nicely and add tomatoes. When the mixture turns thick, add dal and chillies and 2 cups of water. Cook till the curry turns a little thick. Decorate with coriander leaves.

Brinjal Curry

Ingredients (Serves 2)

- 250 grams brinjal, sliced
- 4 red chillies
- 1 tsp. each of coriander seeds, sesame seeds and chana dal
- A pinch of asafoetida
- 10 grams tamarind
- 1/4 tsp. turmeric powder
- 1/4 coconut, grated
- A few curry leaves
- 1/2 tsp. mustard seeds
- Salt to taste

Preparation

Fry chillies, coriander and sesame seeds, coconut and til in little oil to a red colour, then grind this mixture to a coarse paste. Cover tamarind in hot water for 5 minutes and then squeeze out the pulp. Heat 3 tblsps. oil and add mustard seeds. When the seeds stop popping, put in the brinjal slices, curry leaves and salt. Fry until the brinjal slices start changing colour. Add the remaining ingredients. Cook till dry. Pour in 2 cups of water, cook again for 5 more minutes. Decorate with coriander leaves.

Papaya Curry

Ingredients (Serves 6)

- 1 medium raw papaya, peeled and sliced
- 1 medium onion, finely sliced
- 4 green chillies, slit
- 4 flakes of garlic, a 1-inch piece of ginger
- 1 tsp. cumin seeds
- 4 red chillies ,10 peppercorns
- A few curry leaves
- 1/2 coconut
- 1/4 tsp. turmeric powder
- 1 big tomato, grated
- Salt to taste

Preparation

Grind coconut, peppercorns, red chillies, garlic, ginger and cumin seeds to a paste. Heat 2 tblsps. oil and fry the onions lightly. Put in the fried onions, the ground paste, tomatoes and spices, and cook. When oil comes out, add papaya and 1 glass of water. Cook till the papaya is done. Mix in the curry leaves and serve hot.

METHI BHAJI CURRY

Ingredients (Serves 4)

- 1 big bunch fenugreek leaves, cleaned and sliced
- 3 cups of buttermilk
- 1/2 tsp. mustard seeds
- 1/4 tsp. fenugreek seeds
- 4 tsp. gramflour
- 1/4 tsp. turmeric powder
- 1 big onion, minced
- 3 green chillies, minced
- 1 tsp. grated ginger
- Salt and chilli powder to taste

Preparation

Heat 2 tblsps. oil, add fenugreek and mustard seeds. When the seeds stop tossing, add ginger, onion and chillies and fry till soft. Then add to methi, salt, turmeric and chilli powder. Cook till the leaves are done. Mix gramflour in buttermilk and pour in the methi mixture, cook till the gravy is little thick.

METHI AND DAL CURRY

Ingredients (Serves 6)

- 1 cup cooked tuvar dal
- 1 big bunch of fenugreek leaves, cleaned and sliced
- 1 cup finely grated coconut
- 1/2 tsp. mustard seeds
- 1/4 tsp. turmeric powder
- 4 red chillies, broken
- Salt to taste

Preparation

Heat 2 tblsps. oil and put in mustard seeds and chillies. When the mustard seeds stop popping, add methi, salt and turmeric. When the leaves are cooked, add coconut, dal and 2 cups of water. Cook for 5 minutes. Serve hot.

DAL CURRY

Ingredients (Serves 6)

For Dal Diamond

- 250 grams tuvar or arhar dal
- 1 tsp. each of grated ginger and garlic
- 6 green chillies
- Handful of coriander leaves
- 2 medium onions, minced
- Salt and chilli powder to taste

For Curry

- 1 lime-sized ball of tamarind
- 4 red chillies.
- 1 tblsp. coriander seeds
- A few curry leaves
- 2 medium onions
- 2 big tomatoes, grated
- 4 flakes of garlic
- 1/4 tsp. each of mustard and cumin seeds
- 1/4 coconut
- Handful of coriander leaves
- Salt to taste

Preparation

Soak dal in water for a couple of hours. Drain water and grind dal to a coarse paste with ginger chillies, garlic and onions. Mix salt, lime juice and coriander leaves in the dal paste. Make a 1/2 an inch thick layer of the paste in a greased thali. Steam it till it turns firm. Remove from fire, cut into diamond pieces. Deep fry the diamond pieces to a golden colour. Grind coconut, chillies, coriander seeds and garlic to a paste. Heat 2 tblsps. oil and fry the ground paste till oil comes out. Add tomatoes, salt and turmeric powder. Cook till the tomatoes turn soft. In the meanwhile, soak tamarind in hot water for 5 minutes and squeeze out the pulp. Pour tamarind water along with 2 cups of water into the tomatoes. Heat the mixture to boiling, then reduce heat and add the dal pieces. Cook for 5 minutes Heat 2 tblsps. oil and put in mustard and cumin seeds, curry leaves and 2 broken red chillies. When the seeds stop popping, pour the oil mixture over the curry. Decorate with coriander leaves.

DAL KOFTA CURRY

Ingredients (Serves 4)

For Koftas

- 1 cup tuvar or arhar dal
- 1/2 tsp. each of grated ginger and garlic
- 1 small onion
- Handful of coriander leaves
- Salt to taste

For Curry

- 4 cups of buttermilk
- 4 green chillies, slit
- 1/4 coconut, grated
- 1 tsp. grated ginger
- 1 tsp. each of coriander and cumin seeds and chana dal
- 1/4 tsp. fenugreek seeds
- A few curry leaves
- Handful of coriander leaves
- 1/2 tsp. each of mustard seeds and turmeric powder
- Salt to taste

Preparation

Wash and soak dal for a few hours. Drain the water and grind dal to a coarse paste along with ginger, garlic, chillies and onions. Mix salt and coriander leaves in the paste. Form the paste into small balls and steam the balls for 20 minutes. Grind chana dal, coconut, coriander, cumin and fenugreek seeds to a paste. Mix the paste into the buttermilk along with turmeric and salt. Place buttermilk on fire and put in the green chillies and dal koftas. Boil for 2-3 and remove the curry form fire. Heat 2 tblsps. oil and put in mustard seeds and curry leaves. When the seeds stop bursting, pour the oil over curry. Serve decorated with coriander leaves.

VADAIS COCONUT CURRY

Ingredients (Serves 4)

For Vadais

- 2 cups chana dal
- 1/2 cup sliced fenugreek leaves
- 4 small onions, minced
- 4 green chilies, minced
- 4 flakes of garlic, minced
- Salt to taste

For Curry

- 2 cups thick and 3 cups thin coconut milk
- 6 flakes of garlic
- 1 tblsp. poppy seeds
- A few curry leaves
- Handful of chopped coriander leaves
- 2 cardamoms, 8 peppercorns, 2 cloves
- 2 green chillies, minced
- 4 small onions, minced
- 1 tblsp. fried raisins, 12 cashewnuts, fried
- Salt to taste

Preparation

Wash and soak dal in water for a few hours. Drain the water and grind dal to a coarse paste. Mix in all the vadai ingredients. Form the mixture into small round vadas with a hole at the centre on a wet cloth. Deep fry vadas to a golden colour. Grind garlic, poppy seeds and whole spices to a paste. Heat 4 tblsps. oil and fry onions, chillies and curry leaves to a golden colour. Put in the ground paste and fry nicely. Pour on thin coconut milk and bring the mixture slowly to a boil. Reduce heat to simmering and add vadas and remaining spices. Simmer for 2 minutes, pour in thick milk. After 2 minutes, remove the curry form fire and add cashewnuts, raisins and chopped coriander leaves.

VADAI CURD CURRY

Ingredients (Serves 6)

For Vadais

- 250 grams tuvar or arhar dal
- 1 coconut, finely grated
- 6 green chillies
- 1 small bunch of coriander leaves
- 1 tsp. grated ginger
- 1 small onion
- Salt to taste

For Curry

- 250 grams sour curd
- 4 green chillies, slit
- 1 small bunch of coriander leaves
- 1/2 tsp. each of cumin and mustard seeds
- 1-inch piece of ginger
- 1/2 tsp. turmeric powder
- 1 tblsp. urad dal
- 2 tblsp. grated coconut
- Salt to taste

Preparation

Wash and soak dal for a few hours in water. Drain water and grind dal to a coarse paste. Mince together rest of the vadai ingredients and mix with the dal along with salt. Form the minced mixture into round vadais and steam them till firm. Soak urad dal for a few minutes. Drain water and grind dal to a paste along with rest of the curry ingredients. Beat curd with 2 cups of water. Heat 3 tblsps. oil and fry the ground paste till oil comes out. Put the fried paste in curd along with curry leaves, green chillies and salt. Then put in the vadais and simmer for 5-7 minutes. Decorate with coriander leaves.

STUFFED TINDA   SPICY ALLOO CURRY
MALAI KOFTA CURRY   SPICY TINDA

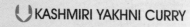

PARSI ALOO
POTATO KOFTA CURRY

KASHMIRI YAKHNI CURRY

11

MANGLOREAN CURRIES

Manglore is near Mysore in Karnataka. This region abounds in coconut trees, therefore coconut is used in almost all Manglorean recipes. Manglorean Christians are non-vegetarians and they prepare well-seasoned and highly spiced meat, chicken, pork, fish, prawn and egg curries which are appetizingly served and enjoyed by a wide section of people.

Non-Vegetarian Curries

Mangalore
Egg Curry

Ingredients (Serves 4)

- 4 hard-boiled eggs, shelled and cut into halves, lengthwise
- 2 medium potatoes, boiled, peeled, cubed and fried lightly
- 4 red and 2 green chillies
- 1/2 tsp. cumin seeds
- 1/4 tsp. turmeric powder
- 1 medium onion
- 1 tsp. each of grated ginger and garlic
- 1 tblsp. vinegar
- 1 tsp. sugar
- 2 big tomatoes, grated
- Handful of sliced coriander leaves
- Salt to taste

Preparation

Grind together ginger, garlic and all the spices to a paste in vinegar. Heat 2 tblsps. oil and fry the ground paste nicely. Put in sugar, salt and tomatoes. Cook the mixture till the tomatoes turn soft. Then put in 2 cups of water, bring the curry to a boil. Reduce heat and put eggs in the curry. Simmer till the gravy turns a little thick. Decorate with coriander leaves.

PRAWN AND BRINJAL CURRY

Ingredients (Serves 6)

- 500 grams prawns, shelled and deveined
- 1 large brinjal, sliced
- 1 tblsp. each of coriander and cumin seeds
- 1/2 tsp. turmeric powder
- 2 tblsp. finely sliced coconut
- 2 big tomatoes, grated
- 2 cups thin and 1 cup thick coconut milk
- 1 big onion, minced
- 1 tsp. each of ginger and garlic paste
- Salt and lemon juice to taste
- Handful of chopped coriander leaves
- Salt to taste

Preparation

Fry sliced onion to a red colour. Powder all the spices. Apply salt and turmeric on prawns and set aside for half an hour. Heat 4 tblsps. oil and put in it onions, garlic and ginger, fry till soft. Add tomatoes and all the spices and cook till dry. Then add prawns, brinjals and thin coconut milk. Cook over a slow fire till the vegetable and prawns are done. Mix in thick coconut milk and remove the curry from fire. Decorate with fried coconut, coriander leaves and sprinkle lime juice on top.

MUTTON CURRY

Ingredients (Serves 5)

- 500 grams mutton, cut into serving portions
- 1 lime-sized ball of tamarind
- 12 small potatoes, 12 small onions
- 2 carrots, 1 large tomato grated
- 250 grams green peas, shelled
- 1/2 tsp. turmeric powder, 1/4 coconut
- 6 red chillies
- 1 tsp. each of ginger and garlic paste
- 1 tblsp. each of cumin and coriander seeds
- 1 big onion, minced
- 1/4 tsp. mustard seeds
- Salt to taste

Preparation

Grind onion, garlic, chillies and all the spices to a paste. Apply the paste on mutton and set it aside for 1 hour. Cover tamarind with hot water for 5 minutes and then squeeze out the pulp. Heat 100 grams oil and fry in it the mutton to a red colour. Cover the fried mutton with hot water. Add salt and tomato and cook till the mutton is half done. Put in the vegetables and tamarind and continue cooking till the mutton and vegetables both are done. Serve hot.

Liver and Potato Curry

Ingredients (Serves 4)

- 500 grams liver, washed and cubed
- 1 lime-sized ball of tamarind
- 2 medium potatoes, boiled, peeled, cubed and fried lightly.
- 2 medium onions
- 4 cloves, 1 small cinnamon stick
- 1/4 coconut
- 6 flakes of garlic
- 1 tsp. cumin seeds
- 1 tblsp. coriander seeds
- 1/2 tsp. mustard seeds
- 1 tsp. anise seeds or saunf
- Salt and chilli powder to taste

Preparation

Cover tamarind with hot water for 5 minutes and then squeeze out its pulp. Grind onion, coconut, garlic and all the spices to a paste. Boil liver in salt water till it becomes tender and dry. Heat 3 tblsps. oil and fry in it the ground paste till oil floats out. Add liver, potatoes and tamarind. Cook for 5 minutes, decorate with coriander leaves.

HOT AND SPICY PORK CURRY

Ingredients (Serves 8)

- 1 kilo pork, cut into serving portions
- 10 red chillies, 1 medium onion
- 1 tsp. turmeric powder
- 1 lime-sized ball of tamarind
- 6 flakes of garlic, 8 peppercorns, 5 cloves
- 1 small cinnamon stick
- 2 tblsps. vinegar, 1 tblsp. sugar, 3 tblsps. brandy
- 150 grams small potatoes, boiled and peeled
- Salt to taste

Preparation

Grind chillies, onion, tamarind, garlic and all the whole spices to make a paste. Heat 100 grams oil and fry in it the ground paste till the oil comes out. Add pork and fry to a golden colour. Then add remaining ingredients except potatoes. Mix well and cover the mixture with boiling water. When the pork is done, put in the potatoes. Cook for a few minutes and remove the curry from fire. Serve hot.

12

MISCELLANEOUS CURRIES

To make this book a true representative of all the famous curries in India, I have given you in this section some famous curries of Rajasthan and Kashmir. Since these regions do not boast of many curries, I had to give your a few select ones for which they are famous. Rajputs are meat-eaters and they are fond of good things in life. Since they lived for long in close contact with Muslims, their curries have a distinct Muslim influence. Only after eating these curries, one marvels at their delicious taste. Besides Rajputs, another dominant community of Rajasthan is Marwaris. They are staunch vegetarians and they use pure ghee in most of their preparations. Marwari food is very simple. But in spite of all the simplicity, their gatta curry has gained national fame. The staple food of Kashmiris is rice which they eat with variety of meat curries. Amongst these curries, Yakhani curry is quite famous. It has a Persian influence on it. Yakhani curry is so delicious that once you eat it, you would like to eat it always. In this section, I couldn't resist including Coorgi mutton curry. It is a class of its own and very delicious.

Safed Mas Curry (Rajasthan)

Ingredients (Serves 4)

- 500 grams mutton, cut into serving portions
- 1/2 cup curd
- 1 tsp. ginger strips
- 2 tblsps. coconut paste
- 1 tsp. white pepper powder
- 1 tsp. white cardamom powder
- 12 cashewnuts, 12 almonds
- 4 tblsps. cream
- Few drops of rose essence
- 100 gms. ghee
- 1 tblsp. lime juice
- Salt to Taste

Preparation

Blanch almonds. Powder 8 almonds and 8 cashewnuts and slice the rest. Parboil mutton. Heat ghee, add mutton, curd, ginger, spice and salt. Cover the mixture with hot water and cook till mutton is tender and one-fourth of the gravy is left. Mix in lime juice, coconut and powdered nuts. Cook for 5 minutes. Remove the curry from fire, mix in rose essence and cream and decorate with nuts.

GATTA CURRY (RAJASTHAN)

Ingredients (Serves 6)

For Gattas

- 2 cups gramflour
- 2 tblsps. ghee
- 1/2 tsp. cumin seeds and turmeric powder
- Salt and chilli powder to taste

For Curry

- 2 cups of sour curd
- 4 green chillies, slit
- 1 tsp. ginger strips
- 1/4 tsp. turmeric powder
- 2 tblsps. gramflour
- 1 tblsp. dhania-jeera powder
- 1/2 tsp. mustard seeds
- A few curry leaves
- Handful of coriander leaves
- Salt and chilli powder to taste
- 2 red chillies, broken

Preparation

Mix all the ingredients of gattas together with very little water to make a firm dough. Make long rolls of the dough and steam the rolls for half an hour. Cut the rolls into round pieces and fry them to a light golden colour. Beat the curd with 1 glass of water and gramflour. Heat 2 tblsps. ghee and add curry leaves, mustard seeds and red chillies. When the seeds stop tossing, add curd mixture, spices and chillies and cook till the curry turns a little thick. Put gattas in the curry and cook for a few more minutes. Decorate with coriander leaves.

MUGHLAI SHAMMI KABAB CURRY

Ingredients (Serves 5)

For Kababs

- 250 grams minced mutton or kheema
- 100 grams kidneys
- 1 egg, 50 grams chana dal
- 1 tsp. ginger and garlic paste
- 4 almonds, 4 cashewnuts, 1 tsp. each of charoli and raisins
- 1 tblsp. garam masala
- Handful of coriander leaves
- 1 onion, minced, a few mint leaves
- Salt and chilli powder to taste

For Gravy

- 100 grams grated onions
- 1 tblsp grated ginger
- 100 grams tomatoes, grated
- 1/8 tsp. saffron strands, soaked in 1 tblsp. hot milk
- 1/2 cup cream
- 25 grams each of pistachios, almonds and cashewnuts, powdered
- 1/2 cup coriander leaves, ground
- 1 tsp. garam masala
- 1 tsp. dhania-jeera powder
- Salt and chilli powder to taste

Preparation

To prepare kababs, soak dal for a few hours. Drain water and boil dal with meat and kidney. Cook till tender and dry. Grind the mixture to a smooth paste. Chop and fry nuts and raisins. Mix the beaten egg and all the kabab ingredients together except nuts. Make balls out of the mixture, place nuts at the centre of each ball. Deep fry balls to a golden colour. Heat 50 grams butter and fry onions and ginger till soft. Add tomatoes and coriander and ground paste of nuts. When the butter separates, put in 2 cups of water. Cook till the gravy turns a little thick. Now pour the curry over kababs. Top it with cream and saffron.

KASHMIRI YAKHNI CURRY

Ingredients (Serves 6)

- 500 grams mutton ribs, cut into serving portions
- 100 grams grated onions
- 1 tsp. each of ginger and garlic paste
- 1/8 tsp. saffron strands, soaked in 1 tblsp. hot milk
- 1/4 litre milk
- 150 grams fresh curd
- 1 tblsp. garam masala
- 1 tblsp. dhania-jeera powder
- 1 tsp. roasted and powdered anise seeds and dry ginger powder
- 25 grams each of almonds and cashewnuts
- Silver warq (option)
- 1 tsp. cardamom powder
- Salt and chilli powder to taste

Preparation

Grind onions, ginger and garlic to a paste. Mix together curd and milk, and strain through a cloth. Boil mutton, strain out the stock and keep the mutton aside. Blanch and grind 3/4th of the nuts, slice the remaining nuts. Heat 50 grams ghee and fry onion, ginger and garlic to a red colour. Add mutton and fry it to a golden colour. Mix in the nuts, stock, milk mixture, spices and salt. When the gravy turns a little thick, remove the curry from fire. Sprinkle sliced nuts and saffron on top. Decorate with warq.

COORGI MUTTON CURRY

Ingredients (Serves 4)

- 500 grams mutton, cut into serving portions
- 150 grams small tomatoes
- 150 grams small potatoes, boiled and peeled
- 250 grams grated onions
- 1 tsp. each of ginger and garlic paste
- 4 green chillies, ground
- 1 tblsp. each of powdered cumin and coriander seeds
- Salt and chilli powder to taste

Preparation

Apply ginger, garlic and chillies to the mutton and set aside for half an hour. Heat 4 tblsps. oil and fry the onions till soft. Add mutton and all the spices and fry to a red colour. Cover the mixture with hot water and cook till the mutton is almost done. Then put in potatoes and tomatoes. When the mutton is cooked, remove the curry from fire. Decorate with coriander leaves and serve hot.

HELPFUL HINTS

1. When preparing fish for fish curry, to remove fish odour from your hands, rub on them vinegar or besan paste or salt.

2. To remove the distinctive fishy smell from the fish, apply on it a mixture of besan, lime juice, turmeric and salt. Set it aside for half an hour, wash well and then put it to cook.

3. To prevent fish from breaking whilst frying, dip it in a light batter of cornflour. This dip will prevent the breaking of the fish slices and even the oil consumption will be much less.

4. To skim fat from chicken and mutton curries, drop in them some ice cubes, you will be surprised to see how the fat gets clinged to the cubes. Then remove the cubes quickly.

5. In order to soften the toughest meat when preparing curries, marinate it with 2 tablespoons sugar for one hour. This way the mutton will not only turn tender but will also have a succulent flavour besides reducing cooking time considerably.

6. If your curry turns very salty, add tomatoes or potatoes to absorb that extra salt

7. To reuse oil in which you have fried fish for preparing curry, add betelnut leaves to the boiling oil. Remove the leaves immediately as they shrink and turn black. The oil will not smell and will become pure again.

8. To remove excessive chillies from your curry, add tomato puree to it or even tamarind juice will do.

9. To give your curry a rich red colour without using too many chillies, soak two red Kashmiri chillies after removing their seeds in half cup of water to which a little vinegar has been added. Blend in the mixer for a second to obtain red colour and add the liquid to the curry.

10. If your curry gets burnt due to oversight, for removing the burnt smell, place a slice of bread on it. Cover the

vessel and keep it aside for a few minutes, then remove the bread.

11. If the vegetables you want to use in the curry have turned stale, soak them for one hour in cold water in which either lime juice or vinegar has been added.

12. If you want to cook rice earlier than the time actually required, and keep it hot, place it in a strainer over gently simmering water and cover with a towel. The rice will remain in perfect condition till your curry is cooked.

India is a home of curries. Here one finds an endless variety of curries, each better than the other. From amongst numerous curries I have chosen for you a wide variety of flavours — so simple to prepare. Some are exotic and some extraordinarily delicious. This book concentrates on curries made in each and every part of India to satiate the palate of those who do not belong to that particular region and yet want to relish every type of curry. So, here is a unique selection of curries which are as distinctive as different wines in different bottles.

IMPORTANT INGREDIENTS USED IN CURRY PREPARATION AND THEIR MEDICINAL VALUE

Garlic

Garlic is a powerful antiseptic, and therefore it kills bacteria. It improves the voice and eyesight. It is a tonic to the hair and is useful in cough, gastric troubles, worms, heart disease, asthma, acidity, piles, chronic fever, loss of appetite, constipation, diabetes and tuberculosis. It also has properties of reducing high blood pressure.

Ginger

Ginger is good for eyes and throat. A small piece of ginger taken with a pinch of black salt before meals eliminates gas. It gives freedom from cough and cold and is also helpful in cardiac disorders, odema, urinary trouble, jaundice, piles and asthma. Ginger juice is also said to prevent the malignancy of the tongue and the throat. Toothache is also relieved if a piece of ginger is rubbed on the painful tooth.

Onions

From the medicinal point of view, white onions are more beneficial to the body than other varieties. They increase virility and induce sleep. They are good for curing tuberculosis, piles, leprosy, swelling and blood impurities. One is saved from sunstroke if one regularly eats raw onions during hot season. Eating raw onion in the morning and at bedtime is good for jaundice patients.

Coriander leaves

Coriander leaves are mostly used for decorating a dish or preparing chutney. They give a special flavour to food. Coriander is not only fragrant and appetizing but also a good digestive aid. It has a cooling effect on our body, and is good for vision and agreeable to the heart.

127

Mint

Mint is usually made into chutneys or sometimes put in non-vegetarian dishes. It is not only palatable and appetizing but is also good for heart. It expels gas and is useful in cough, dysentery, gastroenteritis and diarrhoea.

Vegetables

They are extremely rich source of minerals, enzymes and vitamins. Their nutritional value varies according to their different parts. Leaves, stems and fruits are rich sources of minerals, vitamins, water and roughage, whereas seeds are high in carbohydrates and proteins. Greener and fresher the vegetables, higher their vitamin content. Therefore always go in for fresh vegetables available in the market.

Eggs

Eggs are a valuable source of animal proteins and next to milk in providing nutrition. Egg yolk contains Iron, B vitamins, calcium and a considerable amount of proteins. White portion contains vitamin B and more than half the amount of proteins in egg. Patients of high cholesterol and heart disease should not eat yolks but go only for whites of the egg.

Fish

Fish rates high in nutritional value. It supplies proteins which are more easily digestible than the proteins of meat. Fish gives fat, vitamins A & D and minerals like iodine and copper to the body. Fish is a low-fat form of proteins. Sardines, mackerel and other oily fish contain omega-3 fatty acids that help clear the body of cholesterol.

Meat & Poultry

These are very rich sources of proteins. Besides proteins they are rich in fats, vitamin A and phosphorus. However, kidney and liver are low in fat. Just one helping a day of meat or fish is enough for the daily body requirement of proteins.

FOODGRAINS   Cookery Glossary

English	Spiked millet	Barley	Jowar	Italian millet	Maize (dry)	Oatmeal	Ragi
Hindi	Bajra	Jau	Juar-janera	Kangri	Makai	Jai	Okra
Tamil	Cambu	Barli arisi	Cholam	Thenai	Muka cholam	—	Ragi
Telugu	Gantelu	Barli biyyam	Jonnalu	Korralu	Mekka jonnalu	—	Chollu
Marathi	Bajri	Juv	Jwari	Rala	Muka	Jai	Nachni
Bengali	Bajra	Job	Juar	Syamadhan kangni	Sukna paka bhutta	—	—
Gujarati	Bajri	Jau	Juar	Ral kang	Makai	—	Ragi bhav
Malayalam	Kamboo	Yavam	Cholam	Thina	Unakku cholam	Oat mavu	Moothari (korra)
Kannada	—	—	Jola	—	Vonugida musikinu	Jolu	Ragi
Kashmiri	Baajr'u	Wushku	—	Shol	Makka'y	—	—

Contd...

English	Rice (raw)	Rice (parboiled)	Rice (white)	Rice (black)	Rice flakes	Rice (puffed)	Samai
Hindi	Arwa chawal	Usna chawal	Safed chawal	Chaval (kala)	Chowla	Murmura	Kutki, Sanwali
Tamil	Pachai arisi	Puzhungal arisi	Vellai puttu arisi	Karuppu puttu arisi	Arisi aval	Arisia pori	Samai
Telugu	Pachi biyyam	Uppudu biyyam	Thella biyyam	Nalla biyyam	Atukulu	Murmuralu	—
Marathi	Tandool	Tandool ukda	—	—	Pohe	Murmure	Sava
Bengali	Atap chowl	Siddha chowl	—	—	Chaler khood	Muri	Kangni
Gujarati	Hatna	Ukadelloo chokha	—	—	Pohva	Mumra	—
Malayalam	Pacchari	Puzhungal ari	Velutha puttari	Krutha puttari	Avil	Pori	—
Kannada	Kotnuda	Kotnuda	—	—	Avalukki	—	Puri
Kashmiri	—	—	—	—	—	—	—

Contd...

129

English	Semolina	Vermicelli	Wheat (whole)	Wheat flour (whole)	Wheat flour (refined)	Wheat (broken)
Hindi	Sooji	Siwain	Gehun	Atta	Maida	Daliya
Tamil	Ravai	Semiya	Godumai	Muzhu godmai ma	Maida mavu	Godhumbi ravai
Telugu	Rawa	Semiya	Godhumalu	Godhum pindi	Maidha pindi	Dinchina gadhumalu
Marathi	—	Shevaya	Gahu	Gahu kuneek	Gahu kuneek	Gavache satva
Bengali	Suji	Sewai	Gomasta	Atta	Maida	Bhanga gom
Gujarati	—	—	Ghau	Ato	—	Fadia ghaun
Malayalam	Rava	Semiya	Muzhu gothambu	Gothambu mavu	Maidu tha gothambu mavu	Gothumbu ari
Kannada	—	Shavige	Godhi	Godhi	Hittu madia	Kuttida Godhi
Kashmiri	—	Ku' nu'	—	—	—	—

VEGETABLES

English	Ash gourd	Bitter gourd	Bottle gourd	Brinjal	Broad beans	Cabbage	Capsicum
Hindi	Safed petha	Karela	Chia	Baingan	Sem	Bandhgobi	Simla mirch
Bengali	Chal kumdo	karala	Laoo	Begoon	Sheem	Badha kopee	Lonka
Assamese	Lao bishesh	—	Jati lao	Bengena	Urahi	Bondhakobi	Kashmiri jalakai
Oriya	Pani kakkaru	—	Lau	Baigana	Shimba	Patrokobi	Simla lonka
Marathi	Kohala	Karle	Dudhi	Wangi	Ghewda	Pan kobi	Bhopli mirchi
Gujarati	Petha	Karela	Dudhi	Ringna	Papdi	Kobi	Simla marchan
Telugu	Boodie gumadi	Kakara	Sorakaya	Vankaya	Pedda chikkudu	Kosu	Pedda mirappa
Kannada	Budu gumbala	Hagalkai	Sorekai	Badanekai	Chapparadavare	Kosu	Donne minasinakai
Tamil	Pooshanikkai	Pavakkai	Suraikai	Kaththarikai	Avaraikai	Muttaikosu	Kuda milakai
Malayalam	Kumbalanga	Kaypakka	Cheraikai	Vazhutheninga	Amarakai	Muttakose	Paranji mulagu
Kashmiri	Masha'ly al	Karelu	—	Waangun	—	Bandgobhi	—

Contd...

English:	Carrot	Cauliflower	Cluster beans	Colocasia	Coriander leaves	Cucumber	Curry leaves
Hindi	Gajar	Phulgobi	Guar ki phalli	Arvi	Hara Dhania	Khira	Kadi patta
Bengali	Gujar	Foolcopy	Jhar sim	—	Dhonay pata	Sasha	Curry pata
Assamese	Gajor	Phoolkobi	—	Kochu	Dhania paat	—	Narasingha paat
Oriya	Gajar	Phulakobi	—	—	Dhania patra	—	Bhrusanga patta
Marathi	Gajar	Fulkobi	Govari	Alu kanda	Kothimbir	Kakari	Kadhi patta
Gujarati	Gajar	Fool kobi	Govar	Alvi	Kothmir	Kakdi	Mitho limdo
Telugu	Gajjara	Cauliflower	Gonuchikkudu kayalu	Chamadumpa	Kothimeera	Dosakaya	Karivepaku
Kannada	Gajjari	Hookosu	Gorikayi	Keshave	Kottambari soppu	Southaikayi	Karibevu
Tamil	Carrot	Koveppu	Kothavarangai	Seppann kizhangu	Koththamali ilaigal	Kakkarikkai	Kariveppilai
Malayalam	Carrot	Coliflower	Kothavara	Chembu	Kothamalli ila	Vellari	Kariveppila
Kashmiri	—	Phoolgobhi	—	—	—	Laa'r	—

Contd...

English	Drumstick	French beans	Garlic	Ginger (fresh)	Green chillies	Jackfruit	Lady's finger
Hindi	Sahjan ki phali	Pharsbeen	Lassan	Adrak	Hari mirch	Kathal	Bhindi
Bengali	Sajane dauta	French beans	Rasoon	Ada (tatka)	Kancha lonka	Echore	Dhanroce
Assamese	Sajina	Faras been	Naharoo	Ada (kesa)	Kesa jalakia	—	Bhendi
Oriya	Sajana chhuin	French beans	Rasuna	Ada (kancha)	Kancha lonka	—	Bhendi
Marathi	Shevgyachya shenga	Farasbi	Lasun	Aale	Hirvya mirchya	Kawla phanas	Bhendi
Gujarati	Saragvani shing	Fansi	Lasan	Adu	Lila marcha	Phunas	Bhinda
Telugu	Munagakayalu	French chikkudu	Vellulli	Allam (pachchi)	Pachchi mirapakayalu	Letha panasa	Bendakaaya
Kannada	Nuggekai	Avare	Bellulli	Ashi Shunti	Hasi menasinakai	Yele halasu	Bendekai
Tamil	Murungaikai	Beans	Ulli Poondu	Inji	Pachchai milagai	Pila pinchu	Vendaikai
Malayalam	Muringakkaya	Beans	Veluthulli	Inji	Pachamulagu	Idichakka	Vendakka
Kashmiri	—	—	Ruhan	—	Myool martsu waungun	—	Bindu

Contd...

English	Lettuce	Lemon	Mint leaves	Onion	Parwal	Peas	Plantain flower	Plantain green
Hindi	Salad ke patte	Nimbu	Pudina	Pyaz	Parwal	Matar	Kele ka phool	Kacha kela
Bengali	Lettuce	Lebu	Poodina pata	Pyaz	Potol	Motor	Mocha	Kancha kala
Assamese	Laipaat	Nemu	Podina	—	Patol	Motormah	—	—
Oriya	Lettuce	Lembu	Podana patra	—	Potala	Matar	—	—
Marathi	Saladchi paane	Limbu	Pudina	Kanda	—	Matar	Kel phool	Kele
Gujarati	Lettuce	Limbu	Fudino	Dungli	—	Vatana	Kelphool	Kela
Telugu	Lettuce koora	Nimma	Pudhina koora	Nirulli	—	Bathanedu	Aratipuwu	Arati kayi
Kannada	Lettuce soppu	Nimbu	Pudina sopu	Erulli	—	Betani	Balo mothu	Bala kayi
Tamil	Lettuce keerai	Elumicham pazham	Pudhinaa	Vengayam	—	Pattani	Vazhaippu	Vazhaikkai
Malayalam	Uvarcheera	Cherunaranga	Pudhinaa	Ulli	—	Pattani Payaru	Vazhappoo	Vazhakka
Kashmiri	Salaad	—	—	Gandu	—	Matar	—	—

Contd...

English	Plantain stem	Potato	Radish	Red pumpkin	Ridge gourd	Snake gourd	Sweet potato	Yam elephant
Hindi	Kele ka tana	Aloo	Muli	Sitaphal	Torai	—	Shakarkand	Zaminkand
Bengali	Thor	Aloo	Mulo	Ronga Koomra	Jhinge	Chichinga	Rangalu	Kham aloo
Assamese	—	Alu	—	Ronga lao	—	—	—	Kaath aloo
Oriya	—	Alu	—	Kakharu	—	—	—	Deshi alu
Marathi	Kelecha khunt	Batate	Mula	Lal bhopla	Dodka	Pudwal	Ratale	Suran
Gujarati	Kelanu thed	Batata	Mula	Kolu	Turai	Pandola	Sakkaria	Suran
Telugu	Arati davva	Bangaala dumpa	Mullangi	Erra gummadi	Beerakai	Potlakayi	Dumpalu	Kanda dumpa
Kannada	Dindu	Aalugadde	Mullangi	Kempu kumbala	Heeraikai	Padavalai	Genasu	Suvarnagadde
Tamil	Vazhaithandu	Urulaikizhangu	Mullangi	Parangikai	Pirrkkankai	Podalangai	Sarkarai valli kizhangu	Chenai kizhangu
Malayalam	Vazhappindi	Uralakkizhangu	Mullangi	Chuvappu mathan	Pecchinga	Padavalanga	Chakkara kizhangu	Chena
Kashmiri	—	Oloo	Muj	Paarimal	Turrelu	—	—	—

PULSES

English	Bengal gram (whole)	Bengal gram (split)	Black gram (split)	Black gram (whole)	Cornflour	Cow gram	Green gram (whole)
Hindi	Chana	Chana dal	Urad dal	Sabat urad	Makai ka atta	Lobia (bada)	Moong
Bengali	Chola	Banglar chhola	Mashkolair dal	Mashkolai dal	Bhoottar maida	Barbati	Mug
Assamese	–	Buttor dail	Matir dail (phola)	Matir dail (gota)	Moida	–	–
Oriya	–	Buta (chhota)	Biri (phala)	Biri (gota)	Makka atta	–	–
Marathi	Hurbhura	Chana dal	Udid dal	Udid	Makyache pith	Kuleeth	Mug
Gujarati	Chana	Chana nidaal	Adad ni dal	Adad	Makai no lot	–	Mag
Telugu	Sanagalu	Senaga pappu	Mina pappu	Minu mulu	Mokkajonnalu (pindi)	Ada chandalu	Pesalu
Kannada	Kadale	Kadale bela	Uddina bela	Uddu	Musukinajolada hittu	Thadaguni	Hesaru kalu
Tamil	Muzhu kadalai	Kadalai paruppu	Ulutham paruppu	Ulundhu	Chola Maavu	Karamani	Pachai payaru
Malayalam	Kadala	Kadala parippu	Uzhunnu parippu	Uzhunnu	Cholapodi	Payar	Cherupayaru
Kashmiri	Chanu	–	Maha	–	–	–	Muang

Contd...

English	Green gram (split)	Horse gram	Kesari dal	Kidney beans	Red gram	Red lentils	Soya bean
Hindi	Moong dal	Kulthi	Lang dal	Rajma	Arhar dal	Masoor dal	Bhat
Bengali	–	Kulthi kalai	Khesari	Barbati beej	Arhar dal	Lal masoor (bhanga)	Gari kalai
Assamese	–	–	–	Markhowa urahi	Rahor dail	Masoor dail (phola)	–
Oriya	–	–	–	Baragudi chhuin	Harada dali	Masura dali (phala)	–
Marathi	–	Kuleeth	Lakh dal	–	Tur dal	Masur dal	Soya
Gujarati	–	Kuleeth	Lakh	–	Tuver dal	Masur dal	Soya
Telugu	Pesaru pappu	Ulavalu	Lamka pappu	–	Kandi pappu	Missu pappu	–
Kannada	Hesare bele	Hunuli	–	–	Togar bele	Masur bele	–
Tamil	Pasi paruppu	Kollu	Vattuparuppu	–	Thuvaram parappu	Massor paruppu	–
Malayalam	Cherupayar parippu	Muthira	–	–	Thuvara parippu	Masoor parippu	Soya bean
Kashmiri	–	–	–	–	–	Musur	–

FRUITS AND DRY FRUITS

English	Almond	Coconut	Currants	Dates	Dry plums
Hindi	Badam	Nariyal	Mungaqqa	Khajur	Alu bukhara
Bengali	Badam	Narcole	Manaca	Khejoor	Scokno kool
Assamese	Badam	Narikol	Kismis	Khejur	Sukan bogori
Oriya	Badaam	Nadia	Kala kismis	Khajura	Barakoli jateeya phala
Marathi	Badam	Naral	Manuka	Khajur	Alubhukar
Gujarati	Badam	Naliyer	Kalli draksh	Khajoor	Suka Plum
Telugu	Badam	Kobbari kaaya	Endu nalla dhraksha	Kharjoora pandu	—
Kannada	Badami	Tenginakai	Dweepa dharakshi-kappu	Kharjoora	—
Tamil	Badam/vadhumai	Thengai	Karumdhraakshai	Perichampazham	Aalpacota ular pazham
Malayalam	Badam	Nalikeram/Thenga	Karuthamurthiri	Eethapazham	—

Contd...

English	Guavas	Lemon	Orange	Raisins	Walnuts
Hindi	Amrud	Nimbu	Santra	Kishmish	Akhrot
Bengali	Payara	Lebu	Kamla lebu	Kishmish	Akhrot
Assamese	Madhurium	Nemu	Sumothira	Sukan angoor	Akhrot
Oriya	Piuli	Lembu	Kamala	Kismis	Akhrot
Marathi	Peru	Limbu	Santre	Bedane	Akrod
Gujarati	Jamrukh	Limbu	Santara	Lal draksh	Akhrot
Telugu	Jaamapandu	Nimma	Kamala Pandu	Kismis pallu	Aakrot
Kannada	Seebe	Nimbe	Kittale	Dweepadrakshi	Acrota
Tamil	Koyyapazham	Elumicham pazham	Kichilipazham	Ular dhraakshai	Akhrot
Malayalam	Perakai	Cherunaranga	Madhura naranga	Unakkamunthiri	Akrotandi

DRY SPICES

English	Aniseed	Asafoetida	Basil leaves	Bay leaf	Caraway seeds	Cardamom (brown)	Cardamom (green)	Cinnamon
Hindi	Saunf	Hing	Tulse ke patte	Tej patta	Shahjeera	Moti elaichi	Choti elaichi	Dalchini
Bengali	Mowri	Hing	Tulsi pata	Tej pata	Sajeera	Elach (tamate)	Elach (sobooj)	Daroochini
Assamese	Guwamori	Hing	Tulosi paat	Tejpaat	Bilati jira	Ilachi (muga)	Ilachi (sevija)	Dalcheni
Oriya	Panamahuri	Hengu	Tulasi patra	Teja patra	Sahajira	Aleicha	Gijuratie	Dalachini
Marathi	Badishep	Hing	Tulsichi paney	Tamal patra	Shahjeera	Masala welchi	Welchi (hirvi)	Dalchini
Gujarati	Variyali	Hing	Tulsina pan	Tamal patra	Jiru	Elcho	Lila alchi	Tuj
Telugu	Sopaginja	Inguva	Thulasi akulu	—	Seema sopyginjale	Yalakulu	Yala kulu (pachavi)	Dalchina chekka
Kannada	Sopubeeja	Hingu	Tulasi ele	—	Caraway beejagalre	Yalakki	Yalakki (hasuru)	Dalchini
Tamil	Perumjeerakam	Perungaayam	Thulasi	—	Karunjeerakam	Elakkai (Pazhuppu)	Elakkai (pachchai)	Lavangapattai
Malayalam	Perumjeerakam	Kaayam	Tulasi	—	Karunjeerakam	Elakkaya	Pach Elakkaya	Karuvapatta
Kashmiri	—	Yangu	—	—	—	Aal budu'a aal	—	—

Contd...

English	Cloves	Coriander seeds	Cumin seeds	Fenugreek seeds	Mace	Mustard seeds	Nutmeg	Parsley
Hindi	Laung	Sukha dhania	Jeera	Methi dana	Javitri	Rai	Jaiphal	Ajmooda ka patta
Bengali	Labango	Dhonay	Jeera	Methi	Jaeetri	Sarsay	Jaifall	Parsley
Assamese	Long	Dhania guti	Gota jeera	Paleng	Janee	Sarioh guti	Jaaiphal	Sugandhi lota
Oriya	Labanga	Dhania	Jira	Methi	Jayatree	Sorisha	Jaiphala	Balabalua shaga
Marathi	Lavanga	Dhane	Jire	Methi dane	Jaypatri	Mohari	Jayphal	Ajmoda
Gujarati	Laving	Dhana	Jeeru	Methi	Jaypatra	Rai	Jaypal	Ajmo
Telugu	Lavangalu	Dhaniyalu	Jeelakara	Menthulu	Japathri	Aavaalu	Jaikaaya	Kothimeerajati koora
Kannada	Lavanga	Kottambari beeja	Jeerige	Menthe	Japatri	Sasive kalu	Jaika	Kottambari jotiya soppu
Tamil	Kraambu	Koththamali virai	Jeerakam	Vendhayam	Jaadipathri	Kadugu	Jaadhikai	Kothamalu ilaigal pole
Malayalam	Karayaamboovu	Kothamalli	Jeerakam	Uluva	Jathipathri	Kadugu	Jathikka	Malliela pole
Kashmiri	Ru'ang	Daaniwal	Zyur	—	Jalwatur	—	Zaaphal	

Contd...

English	Peppercorns	Pomegranate seeds	Poppy seeds	Red Chillies	Tamarind	Turmeric	Vinegar	Thymol
Hindi	Kali mirch ke daane	Anardana	Khus khus	Lal mirch	Imli	Haldi	Sirka	Ajwain
Bengali	Marich	Dareem bij	Posto	Paka lonka	Tentool	Halood	Seerka	—
Assamese	Jaluk	Dalim guti	—	Sukan jalakia	Teteli	Halodhi	Sirika	—
Oriya	Golamaricha	Dalimba manji	—	Nali lankamaricha	Tentuli	Haladi	Vinegar	—
Marathi	Kale Miri	Dalimbache dane	Khas khas	Lal mirchya	Chincha	Halad	Sirka	Onva
Gujarati	Mari	Dadamna bee	Khaskhas	Lal marcha	Amli	Haldar	Sirko	—
Telugu	Miriyaalu	Daanimma ginjalu	Gasagasaalu	Erra mirapa kayalu	Chinthapandu	Pasupu	—	—
Kannada	Menasina kalu	Dalimbo beeja	Gasagase beeja	Kempu menasinakai	Hunase hannu	Arasina	—	—
Tamil	Milagu	Maadhulai vidhai	Kasakasaa	Milagai vatal	Puli	Manjal	Pulikaadi	—
Malayalam	Kurumulagu	Madhala naranga kuru	Kaskas	Chuvanna Mulagu	Puli	Manjal	Vinagiri	—

136

Safe-n-Sure •
Weight Loss Programme

—Pankaj Sharma &
Dr. Ashok Gupta

This self-help weight loss book is probably India's *first well-defined programme on losing weight positively and naturally.* The book includes information on other weight loss regimens in the market and discusses their pitfalls.

Following the *Safe-n-Sure Weight Loss Programme* also ensures you don't regain the lost weight after some time. This step-by-step programme includes an exercise regimen and crucial information on food and diet, with an exclusive chapter on low-calorie recipes, vegetarian as well as non-vegetarian. All of which makes this book a truly holistic weight loss guide that will help you lose weight *safely* and *naturally,* and *maintain* your ideal weight thereafter.

Demy Size • Pages: 132
Price: Rs. 96/- • Postage: Rs. 15/-

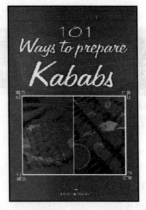

101 Chinese Recipes

—Aroona Reejhsinghani

Indians are crazy about Chinese food. Since majority of the people love Chinese food, most of the restaurants serve it. Considering this craze the author has brought out her third book on Chinese food for you. In this book she has given you a great variety of Chinese dishes ranging from the hot favourites like fried rice, Manchurian, chilly chicken to the exotic like cloud swallows, steamed bao-tse, fragrant chicken, Chinese mixed grill to many other delightfully delicious dishes.

Get ready to enter the world of exotic Chinese culinary delights!

Demy Size • Pages: 112
Price: Rs. 60/- • Postage: 15/-

101 Ways to Prepare Kababs

—Satarupa Banerjee

Kabab has always taken the pride place on Indian cuisine. It has variety and class.

In this book, the author describes the simple process for preparing kababs from meat, chicken, fish, paneer vegetables, fruits etc. Several cooking methods of kababs have also been described including the dressing, roasting and presenting. It includes preparation in the tandoor, tawa, kadahi, handi, patila, over hot coals and in the oven, grill or microwaves.

Explained in easy-to-follow language to facilitate easy preparation, the book describes how both the vegetarians and non-vegetarians can enjoy and relish kabab—ranging from sweet to savoury or from spicy to fruity. Here for you is a distinctive selection of delicious kababs. Enjoy and pamper yourself with the culinary delights of kababs.

Demy Size • Pages: 136
Price: Rs. 60/- • Postage: 15/-

Dishes and Desserts

—*Tanushree Podder*

Pamper yourself with the culinary delights

From the green valley and the gurgling streams of Kashmir down to the Malabar coast, the western ghats to the eastern horizon, India has a variety of culinary delights which are a treat to a gourmand's palate.

Indian Cuisine has been deeply influenced by the Mughals, Nizams, Portuguese, Dutch and the English who have enriched it and lent a unique aroma and flavour. The succulent *kababs,* the tongue-tickling taste of stuffed *paranthas, sarson ka saag, makki ki roti, khaman dhokla, farsan, puran poli, idli, dosa* and *sambar,* each lend a distinctive taste and rule the roost in most restaurants and hotels.

Indian Cuisine gives you a number of recipes from across the country which make the tongues drool with excitement. Both vegetarian and non-vegetarian delights are included along with a number of lip-smacking desserts.

Big Size • Pages: 104
Price: Rs. 80/- • Postage: Rs. 15/-

Cooking for Diabetics

—Satarupa Banerjee

Diet plays a very important role for any disease, more so for diabetes

There was a time when diabetic diet meant uninspiring tasteless food. Thankfully the diet scene for the diabetics is no longer gloomy or bland as it used to be.

Within a few restrictions, diabetic food is definitely a gourmet fare now. This book will show how diabetic food can not only benefit the patient but lead the way for a healthy lifestyle that the whole family will benefit from.

Demy Size • Pages: 115
Price: Rs. 80/- • Postage: 15/-

Over 100 Fat-Free Recipes

—Elizabeth Jyothi Mathew

With fast food and junk foods being the order of the day, thanks to our rushed modern existence, staying healthy is of prime importance. More often than not, we forego some of the most delicious food in order to stay healthy. It is not necessary to give up culinary delicacies to maintain good health. This book shows just how.

The author discloses dishes that are nutritious as well as low in calories and high on taste. This book takes readers on a journey of culinary experimentation with different recipes that can then be incorporated into a healthy lifestyle. The recipes are divided into four sections: Vegetable Dishes, Meat and Poultry Dishes, Seafood Dishes and Desserts. These calorie-counted recipes will help you maintain a diet that includes various types of food, ensuring all your nutritional requirements are met. So, eat well and stay slim and healthy with *Over 100 Fat-free Recipes.*

Demy Size • Pages: 120
Price: Rs. 96/- • Postage: 15/-

101 Ways to Prepare Soups & Salads

—Aroona Reejhsinghani

A steaming hot bowl of soup or a bowl of fresh and crisp vegetables can be had both as an appetiser or as a whole meal. As people are discovering the goodness of wholesome foods, soups and salads have become perennial favourites and are being accepted as an integral part of the usual lunch or dinner.

101 Ways to Prepare Soups and Salads helps you in discovering new methods of preparation of appetizing and stimulating soups and salads, both light and elaborate ones, for the consumption of the whole family.

Soups and salads from around the world:

❖ Cold soups ❖ Non-vegetarian, Vegetable soups ❖ Vegetarian, Moulded salads ❖ Seafood salads ❖ Fruit and nut salads

Demy Size • Pp: 86
Price: Rs. 60/-
Postage: Rs. 15/-

101 Mix & Match Recipes with Vegetables

—Satarupa Banerjee

A lot has been said in recent times about a vegetarian diet. Including vegetables in our diet is, of course, extremely beneficial.

But **101 Mix & Match Recipes with Vegetables** is not for the strict vegetarians. It is for the diehard non-vegetarians who can mix meat, fish and eggs with assorted vegetables and get the best of both the worlds.

The author believes that a little animal protein mixed with vegetables makes for a better balanced meal. The book shows how a judicious combination of vegetables and animal protein produces delicious results.

Demy Size • Pp: 143
Price: Rs. 60/-
Postage: Rs. 15/-

101 All Time Savoury Snacks

—Elizabeth Jyothi Mathew

"Whether therefore you eat or drink or whatsoever you do, do all to the glory of God."
— 1 Corinthians 10:31

Creamy mushrooms on toast, potato scones, pineapple sandwiches, cheese biscuits, eggs florentine, deep-fried king prawn, omelette pizza, favourite quiche.

These and more tantalising, lip-smacking recipes have been included in this book to help you churn out a whole array of tempting, tasty and nutritious dishes for your children for those in-between times.

Demy Size • Pp: 102
Price: Rs. 60/-
Postage: Rs. 15/-

Modern Cookery Book

A must for every housewife

—Asha Rani Vohra

Praises are showered on a gourmet who can churn out good dishes as well as present it well on the table.

The modern housewife is a very conscious lady and wants to move with the times. She wants to do her work better with the help of scientific equipments, technological ways and means, and give her work an artistic touch, thus saving her labour and time.

This book attempts to cater to not only the metropolitan housewives but also the small-town housewives. In order to acquaint them about how to organise parties, the etiquettes to be observed and the presentation of the food are all given for the benefit of the readers.

Apart from culinary delights from across the world, the book includes sections on:

❖ Ideal kitchen
❖ Art of serving and table decoration
❖ Table manners

Demy Size • Pages: 144
Price: Rs. 60/- • Postage: Rs. 15/-